WALES HISTORY

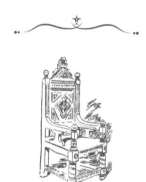

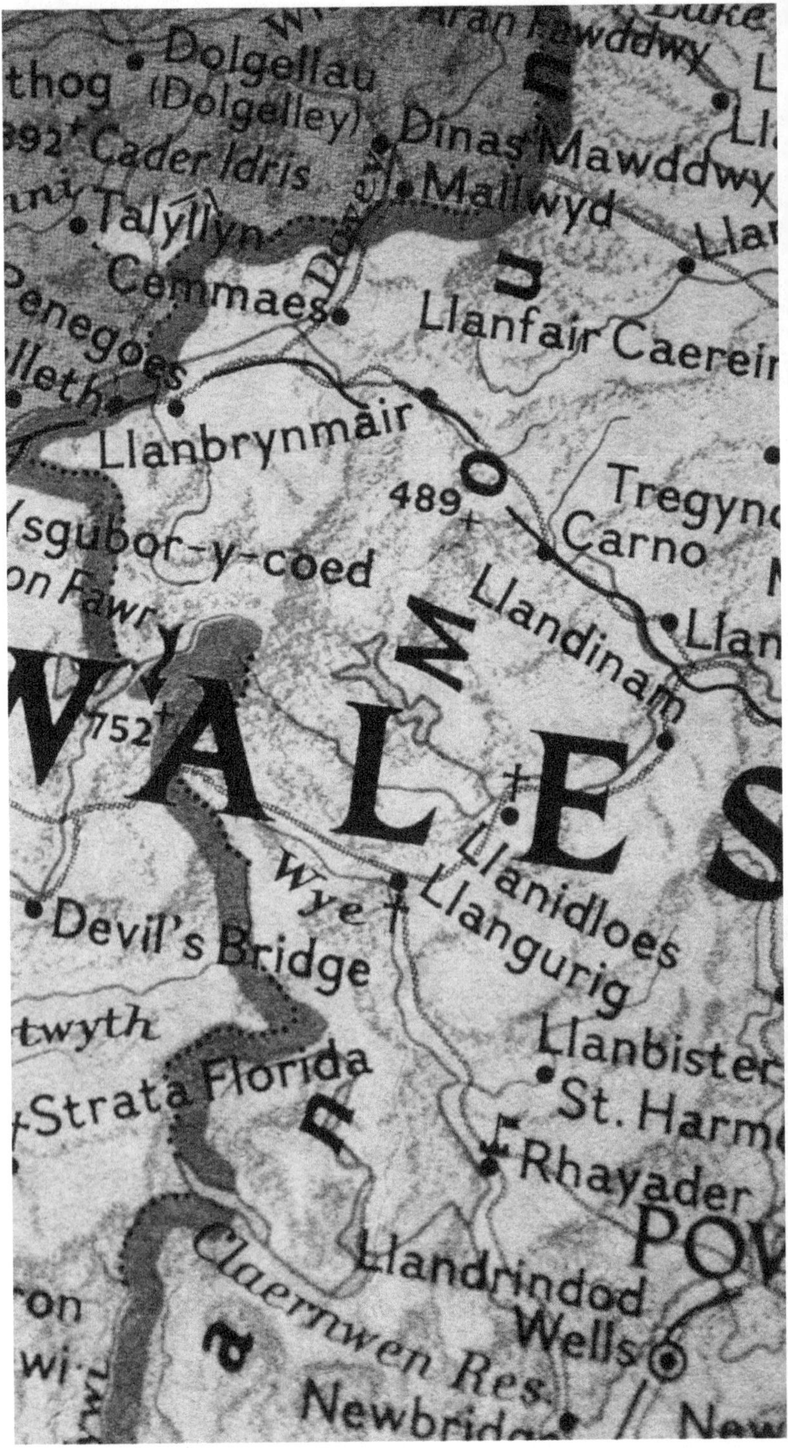
Dolgellau
(Dolgelley)
Cader Idris
Talyllyn
Dinas Mawddwy
Mallwyd
Cemmaes
Llanbrynmair
489
Carno
Llandinam
752
WALES
Wye
Llanidloes
Llangurig
Devil's Bridge
Strata Florida
Llanbister
Rhayader
Llandrindod
Wells
Claerwen Res

WALES HISTORY

FREE BONUS FROM HBA: EBOOK BUNDLE

Greetings!

First, thank you for reading our books.

Now, we invite you to join our VIP list. As a welcome gift we offer the History & Mythology eBook Bundle below for free. Plus, you can be the first to receive new books and exclusives! Remember it's 100% free to join.

Simply click the link below to join.

https://www.subscribepage.com/hba

Keep up to date with us on:
YouTube: History Brought Alive
Facebook: History Brought Alive
www.historybroughtalive.com

CONTENTS

INTRODUCTION

Nestling between rugged mountains and sweeping coastlines lies a land steeped in legend and lore, where the echoes of centuries past resonate in every valley and hillside. This is Wales, a unique nation that is as rich and varied as its rugged landscape. From the ancient Celts who left such a mark on its history and culture to the bustling modern cities of today, Wales has a colourful history to discover as it has witnessed the rise and fall of kingdoms and the clash of empires. Through all these difficult times, the Welsh continued to forge their own strong and incomparable national identity.

Wales (Cymru) is one of the four countries in the United Kingdom. Wales is known for its beautiful countryside that is dotted with castles and other fortifications that are the legacy of the country's long and rich history. Wales is situated in the western part of Great Britain and is surrounded on three sides by water, with its border with England running down its eastern side. Wales is not a large country, as it has an area covering just 20,779m². Nevertheless, it is a memorable one with valleys, misty mountains and dramatic rocky coastlines. Its people are rightly proud of their Welsh heritage and it is something they have fought hard to maintain over the centuries.

The story of Wales begins many centuries ago in prehistoric times. Archaeologists have discovered that the first footprints on Welsh soil were made by pre-Celtic tribes. During the Iron Age, the country saw the emergence of Celtic tribes that would not only leave their distinctive mark on the countryside, but also on its culture.

Britain was invaded by the Romans in the 1st century AD. They marched westwards to Wales and swept the country into the Roman Empire. The Romans left their marks on the country as during their occupation, they constructed excellent roads, forts and settlements. Notable sites like Caerwent and Caerleon were built and can still be seen today.

Following the fall of the Roman Empire, Wales witnessed the incursions of the Anglo-Saxons and other Germanic tribes. This era was marked by political fragmentation and saw the emergence of many native Welsh kingdoms - each one vying for supremacy. The story of Wales is one of resilience and resistance, as the Welsh people stood firmly against both the Roman invaders and Norman conquerors, fiercely defending their language, culture, and way of life.

It was during the Mediaeval period that Wales became a nation in its own right, with the Welsh princes ruling from powerful castles like Caernarfon and Harlech. Wales was caught in the middle between ambitious English kings and the bitter rivalries of its own princes. Despite all the conflict, this was a time that was rich in music, poetry and dance. The situation culminated in the conquest of much of the country by Edward I and this resulted in much of Wales being brought under English law.

As well as conflict and conquest, the history of Wales is also defined by the steadfast determination of its people to preserve their identity and traditions. Throughout the centuries of English domination that followed, the Welsh language has endured and is still proudly spoken by millions of people across the country. From the industrial heartlands of South Wales to the remote rural communities of the north, Wales remains a nation united by its common heritage and a strong sense of belonging.

As the 20th century drew to a close, it marked a new chapter in the history of Wales. 1999 saw the devolution of powers to the National Assembly for Wales (Senedd Cymru) and the promise of more significant social and political changes for the country. Today, Wales remains a proud and now independent nation within the United Kingdom that embraces its own unique and vibrant history and culture.

Every year more than one million visitors explore the beautiful landscapes of Wales and discover the country's colourful cultural tapestry. They find that  Wales is steeped in history at every turn. From the peaks of Snowdonia to the sandy beaches of the Gower peninsula, there are traces of the country's history and visitors soon become immersed in its vivid myths and legends.

You too can make this fascinating journey. Join me now as we embark on a journey through the centuries where the country's ancient landscapes resonate with the words of the Welsh national anthem 'Hen Wlad Fy Nhadau" - "Land of my Fathers" – which reveals the passionate and enduring spirit of its people.....

CHAPTER 1
ANCIENT BEGINNINGS

The story of Wales begins millions of years ago, during the last Ice Age, when massive sheets of ice covered much of the Northern Hemisphere. Glaciers sculpted the Welsh landscape and left behind numerous iconic features that can still be seen today. Such classic glacial features as u-shaped valleys, cirques, and rugged mountainous terrain, demonstrate the force of the glaciers that shaped the hills and valleys of Wales.

The geography of Wales has changed very little since then and the features carved by the glacial ice can still be seen today. The country has a mountainous backbone with Snowdonia in the north-west which includes the five peaks of Mt Snowdon. At 1,085m (3,560 feet) Yr Wyddfa, is the highest of these peaks and the highest in Wales. The Brecon Beacons in the south of the country have been carved from red sandstone with Pen y Fan (886m/ 2,906 feet) being its highest peak.

The best place to study the features of glaciation is the Snowdonia National Park, which is home to Mount Snowdon. The park showcases all the classic features of glaciation including pyramidal peaks, striated rock surfaces, and glacial moraines.

Earliest civilisations

The earliest civilisations in Wales pre-date the arrival of the Celts, but information about them is shrouded in mystery because of limited archaeological evidence. These early inhabitants are often referred to as 'pre-Celtic' or the indigenous people of Wales and their communities evolved over several millennia. There are scant remnants of their existence, so it is hard for historians and archaeologists to give a comprehensive narrative of their lives. Nonetheless, ongoing research and archaeological excavations continue to provide more insight into the ancient communities of Wales.

The oldest archaeological find

The oldest artefact found to date is believed to be 230,000 years old. It is a jawbone of the Neanderthal species of humans that was found in the Valley of Elwy in Northern Wales. Excavations that took place in the Pontnewydd Cave which is situated near St Asaph uncovered simple stone tools as well as some human teeth – both are now exhibited in the National Museum of Wales.

One of the prominent pre-Celtic groups who lived in ancient Wales was closely linked with the Beaker culture, which was named after their distinctive pottery vessels. This culture emerged during the late Neolithic and early Bronze Age (2,500 BC – 1,800 BC). The Beaker people are believed to have originated from continental Europe - possibly from the Iberian Peninsula. They were talented and introduced the use of bronze for making hand tools and weapons. Archaeological sites including Penywyrlod in Powys and Gaer Fawr in Pembrokeshire have both revealed artefacts that are characteristic of the Beaker culture and also revealed their burial traditions. It is believed that Wales was not continuously inhabited until about 9,000BC.

Mesolithic habitants

Another pre-Celtic group that habited Wales in ancient times is associated with the Mesolithic period (8,800BC - 4,500BC) and marked by the construction of huge stone structures. Wales has numerous megalithic sites, some of which can be explored today. with burial chambers and standing stones. A number of ancient burial chambers, standing stones, and stone circles are dotted across the Welsh landscape. Pentre Ifan, is a Neolithic burial chamber in Pembrokeshire. These sites give archaeologists a greater understanding of the community's rituals, spirituality, and possibly its social structure.

The Iron Age

The Iron Age in Wales began around 700 BC and saw the construction of numerous hill forts as cultural and defensive centres. The people of

 this era are often referred to as the Celtic tribes (more about the Celtic period in Chapter 2), although their distinct identities and cultural practices varied across regions. The hill fort at Tre'r Ceiri on the Llŷn Peninsula is one of the most well-preserved and impressive examples, offering insights into the organisation of Iron Age societies in Wales.

Archaeological evidence suggests there was a degree of continuity between the pre-Celtic and Celtic periods; challenging the idea that there was an abrupt cultural shift. It is likely that the indigenous people interacted with incoming Celts rather than experiencing a displacement.

The Celtic tribes are thought to have originated from central Europe and their migration westward brought changes in language, social structures and artistic expression.

CHAPTER 2
THE ARRIVAL OF CELTS

The Celts were a number of groups of Indo-European people who shared similarities in their culture and language. They formed an extensive network right across ancient Europe. The term "Celts" is usually used to describe these various tribes and communities rather than referring to a single, homogenous group. The name Celt came from the Greek word Keltoi and the Roman Celtai, and was used to describe 'people of continental Europe' who were neither Greeks or Romans.

The Celts emerged in the late Bronze Age and Iron Age, with their influence spanning from the 8th century BC to the Roman conquests in the 1st century AD. The origin of the Celts is complex and some historians believe they originated in central Europe. Importantly, by the 8th century BC, Celtic-speaking groups had begun to expand across Europe, reaching as far west as the Iberian Peninsula, east to Anatolia, and northwards to the British Isles.

All parts of the island of Britain that lay south of the Firth of Forth, were inhabited by Celts who spoke versions of the same language – Brittonic. The Celts lived in Wales from 600BC until AD43 when the Roman Invasion of Northern Wales took place. In England, the Celts established various tribal societies. Notable among these were the Britons, who inhabited much of what is now England, and the Belgae, who settled in the south-east of England. The Celts were well-established in England by the time of Julius Caesar's expeditions in the 1st century AD.

The Celtic migration into Wales occurred during the Iron Age, with evidence suggesting a gradual and steady movement rather than a sudden influx. The exact timing and mechanisms of this migration remains unknown but archaeological findings, linguistic analysis, and historical accounts indicate that the Celts entered Wales over several centuries, starting around the 7th century BC. A number of Celtic tribes started to emerge in Wales- each with its own distinct identity and culture.

By the time the Romans began their

occupation of Britain, the Celts in Wales had established a mosaic of different tribal communities, each contributing to the rich tapestry of Welsh history.

Who were the Celts?

Celtic history has significantly coloured the heritage and culture of Wales – and also Scotland and Ireland. The Celts were strong and brave warriors, who believed in spirits found in the Welsh mountains, forest, rivers and springs.

The Celts lived in four main tribes in Wales: The Ordovices were mainly in the north-west, the Deceangli in the north-east, the Silures were located in the south-east and the Demetae in the south-west.

The different tribes in Wales had the same language and traditions as other Celtic tribes in Britain. The Celts built hill forts which they surrounded with deep ditches to protect them and lived in clans – extended families. Their houses were round and made of wattle and daub with dirt floors and pitched thatched roofs. The Celts were surprisingly sophisticated and used early forms of combs, razors and hair decorations. They were also religious, worshipping many different gods.

Celtic art

The Celts were very artistic and made many beautiful stone carvings and intricate metal work. Celtic designs in precious metals can be found in museums. Celtic  art gives a good insight into how they viewed their surroundings and their gods. The style of Celtic art found in Wales is called La Tène art and developed from 500 BC onwards. Some excellent examples of this can be seen in the National Museum in Cardiff.

The earliest example of Celtic art found in Wales is the Cerrig-y-Drudion bowl which was found in a grave in the county of Conwy in 1924. Interestingly, the grave had been lined with stone. Some of the designs used in Celtic art appear very frequently. The moon-shaped plaque from Llyn Cerrig Bach is decorated with an elaborate belletrist – a three-legged design, with the legs radiating from a central point. The belletrist is thought to represent the relationship between the living, the dead and the gods.

Celtic hill forts

There are more than 1,000 Celtic hill forts

to be seen today in Wales. Some of them are just outlines on hilltops, but one of the most fascinating is Castell Henllys, which has scale reconstructions of Iron Age roundhouses and runs a series of workshops with Iron Age themes. The site is located in beautiful woodland near Nevern in the Pembrokeshire National Park. (Pembrokeshire Coast National Park, 2024b) (Pembrokeshire Coast National Park, 2024c)

Among the best hill forts to see in Wales are:

- Castell Dinas Bran (near Llangollen in North Wales)
- Gaer Fawr near Welshpool in Mid Wales. Excavations
- Ffridd Faldwyn near Montgomery in Powys, mid-Wales
- For a full list of hill forts in Wales, refer to the following list.

(Wikipedia contributors, 2023)

Religion

The Celts were religious and revered many gods. They would hold religious ceremonies in woods and near sacred water. They firmly believed that a person's spiritual power was in their head so it was considered the greatest trophy to have the head of their enemy which they would proudly hang on their door.

Druids

There has been a great deal of folklore about the Druids. They were an important part of Celtic culture and their focus in Wales was the island of Anglesey. Druids were high-class priests and advisers who taught, healed and mediated. They had their own centres of learning where all knowledge was passed down from one generation to the next. Certain Druids were extremely powerful and they would be ambassadors for warring clans and were the ones to maintain the law.

Further reading:
https://museum.wales/articles/1341/Who-were-the-Celts/
https://www.britainexpress.com/wales/history/iron-age.htm

The Celtic language

The native tongue of Wales is Welsh which has its roots in the Celtic language and is one of the oldest languages in the world - along with Ancient Greek and Latin. There are 29 letters in the Welsh alphabet and there are two additional vowel sounds - W and Y. In recent years, there has been a revival in the use of the Welsh language and today, it is widely spoken with one in five people living in Wales, speaking Welsh - which equates to 16% of the population. Welsh schoolchildren are taught Welsh as part of their curriculum.

Welsh shares the same linguistic roots of Brittonic as Breton spoken in Brittany and Corning, the native language of Cornwall. Brittonic was spoken in ancient times across the island of Britain. Welsh only has a few similarities with Irish Gaelic so the written and spoken languages sound quite different. The Welsh language really became distinctive between 400- 700 AD and the oldest known poems in Welsh, date from this period.

Wales today is very much a bilingual country. Almost all signs including road signs are written in both English and Welsh, and most schools and organisations in Wales promote the use of Welsh language'.

Ceryn   Evans   in
https://www.twinkl.fr/blog/10-fascinating-welsh-language-facts

The modern Welsh name for Wales is Cymru and its people, Cymry. Both of these words come from the Brythonic word 'combrogi', meaning 'fellow-countrymen' and both were in use well before the 7th century.

Interesting facts about the Celts

- The Celts wore brightly-coloured clothing and some drew patterns on their skin using the blue dye from woad plants.
- The style of clothing they wore showed their status within the clan.
- The Celts are said to have been the first people in Europe to wear trousers and these were fastened by clasps called fibuales.
- They foraged for wild plants, berries and mushrooms and hunted for deer, foxes and badgers. The Celts fished and they also reared domestic animals. They would eat eggs from domestic hens as well as wild birds. One of the Celtic inventions was the iron plough which

was much stronger than earlier ploughs made from sticks, so could be used on much heavier soils which included the fertile soils of the Welsh valleys.

- The Celts did not call themselves 'Celts' but they were commonly called by the name of their tribe rather than by one collective name.

- Women were considered equal to men and could own property and choose their own husbands. They could also lead in war as Queen Boadicea did. If a woman had children, she would not raise them herself because this was the job of foster parents.

The legacy of the Celts

The Celts had a significant impact on Wales and their legacy can be found in many aspects of the country's rich history, culture and language.

The Welsh Language

The Welsh language (Cymraeg) has evolved from the language spoken by the ancient Celts in the region and has played an important role in preserving the Welsh national identity.

Celtic art and design

Celtic art and its rich use of symbols has influenced Welsh arts, crafts and jewellery to this day. As well as symbols, the Celts used intricate knotwork and made patterns by lacing threads and examples of these designs can be found in many pieces of Welsh artwork.

Celtic mythology

The Celtic pagan religion was rich in mythology and this has influenced Welsh folklore and legends over the centuries.

Welsh place Names

Many place names in Wales have Celtic origins and reflect the fact that they were once Celtic settlements.

Culture and traditions

Welsh music, dance and storytelling have all been influenced by the country's Celtic heritage. Traditional Welsh music often features Celtic instruments and melodies.

Ethnic Identity

The Welsh national identity has been strongly influenced by its Celtic roots. The Welsh are proud of their rich cultural heritage and unique language and know that they are closely connected to the Celtic legacy in Wales.

CHAPTER 3
THE ROMAN INVASION

During the first century AD, Britain was invaded by the Romans and the Celts they encountered became known as 'Britons' by them. In AD43, the Romans began a campaign to bring the whole island of Britain totally under Roman rule. The Romans believed this would be easy as they had swept through southern England, but when they reached the Welsh borders a few years later, they found the mountains challenging and the Celtic tribes ready to fight the conquering army. The Roman conquest of Wales was to prove to be a long and

brutal period in the country's history, lasting about 30 years. It is interesting to note that Wales was never totally conquered.

The Romans captured north-eastern Wales, defeating the Deceangli (known as Tegeingl in Welsh) in AD 48. The Deceangli were a Celtic tribe that lived in hill forts in the area where the city of Chester is situated today. Roman silver and lead mine workings have since been found in this area.

In AD50, the Romans defeated the Ordovices. This Celtic tribe had extensive lands in North Wales. The Celts fought the Romans hard for 20 years- much of this time was under their leader, Caractacus, who organised the Welsh resistance. Caractacus was the son of the king of the Catuvellauni in Essex and had led the British campaign against the Romans. He had however, been forced to flee with many of his warriors when he was defeated in battle near the River Medway.

Caractacus had become the leader of the Ordovices and Silures tribes in Wales, but was defeated in battle in AD50. He was captured and sent to Rome. The Ordovices had to accept defeat when their final stronghold for both Celts and Druids in Anglesey was captured by the Romans in AD61. Wales was finally brought under the control of the Roman Empire.

'Their aim was to grow the Roman Empire by using Wales's natural resources, people, and farmland'. (HWb, n.d.)

Life under Roman rule

The Romans divided the land of Wales into lowland areas for the people and highland areas as military zones. They also established three major fortresses at York, Chester and Caerleon in Wales. The Roman establishment at Caerleon was designed with the classic Roman layout and was completed in AD78, with a sizable fortified town, which the Romans named Isca. This was to become the most important Roman site in Wales with an army of more than 5,500 men. The town had bath-houses with heated water, a hospital and an amphitheatre for regular combat with gladiators. The amphitheatre had seating for 6,000 people. Today, Caerleon is one of the best remaining military sites and is situated close to the River Usk, near Newport.

The construction of Roman forts

From Isca, the Romans developed a network of at least 30 smaller forts that stretched westwards and northwards to the island of Anglesey. The forts were linked by roads and the location of the forts ensured that they were only one day's march from each other. Military stations were also established near Caerleon and these included ones at Abergavenny, Monmouth, Neath and Loughor. The result was the establishment of an uneasy peace between the Romans and the Celts. Several of the Celtic clans in time did become Romanised.

The Romans were not particularly interested in Wales because they found its geography difficult and there was little flat and easily cultivated land. The area that they developed more than any other was south-east Wales. There were towns created and villas built in the countryside. The new forts were the focus of trade and new communities grew up around them- all with bustling markets. The largest markets sold goods from all over the Roman Empire. The Roman government was divided into administrative areas called civitates which were self-governing.

The introduction of Roman law...

There were two civitates in Wales at

Carmarthen and Caerwent- which was situated just east of Caerleon. With a population of more than 3,000, Caerleon was the biggest town in Wales. The Romans did allow the Celtic ruling classes to keep their lands and customs- as long as they also supported Roman law. The Celts could also continue working on their farms. The classic round houses remained the normal type of housing, although it is estimated that 1% of the Romans lived in luxurious villas.

...And the Latin language

One of the biggest changes was that Latin became the official language of Wales, but unlike in many other European countries, Latin did not replace the native language. The majority of the Welsh continued to speak their Brythonic Celtic language. Latin became the language of the aristocracy. Brythonic did change during the Roman occupation because many Latin words were absorbed into the language. Examples of this include fort, rooms and books and these words can still be found in modern Welsh.

'The Romans brought with them different food, plants, animals, public baths, medicine, doctors, and religions. In their society, the elite learnt to read and write. The Iron Age population of Wales became "Romanised" as they took on this new culture' (HWb, n.d.-b)

Once Roman rule had been established in Wales, there is little mention of the country during the next 100 years, as the focus was on other places in the Roman Empire. In the third century, Emperor Septimius decided to divide Britain into two parts and Wales became part of Britannia Superior and was controlled from London. In AD412 Roman citizenship was given to every freeman in Wales. During the 4th century, the country was becoming prosperous but within 100 years, this was to change as the Roman Emperor began to deploy his armies elsewhere in the Empire.

In AD410, the Roman emperor Honorius decided to withdraw all Roman troops from Britain province to defend other parts of the empire. All this marked the end of Roman rule of Britain, it also left the island vulnerable to attacks from various groups - including the Anglo-Saxons and the Picts.

Interesting facts about the Romans

- The Romans spoke Latin, but many of them also spoke Greek.
- Roman armies were extremely well trained and disciplined and regularly defeated larger armies.
- Roman rulers would consume a small quantity of poison every day to help strengthen their immune systems.
- Bathing was a communal activity and everyone would get into huge baths to

cleanse themselves. The Roman Baths at Caerleon (Isca) could hold 80,000 gallons (300,000 litres) gallons of water.

- The favourite sport of the Romans was gladiator fights. These took place in amphitheatres like the one at Caerleon which had wooden benches that could accommodate 6,000 spectators. As well as two gladiators fighting, often the entertainment was to watch a gladiator fight a large exotic animal.
- The Romans were clever and the first to invent many things including concrete, books, the Julian calendar, first heating system for buildings and aqueducts.

(Pwpadmin, 2023)

The Roman legacy

The Roman legacy to Wales is testament to the enduring influence of one of the greatest civilisations in history. The Romans left an indelible mark on Wales, shaping its landscape, culture and society for many centuries to come.

Travelling through Wales there is plenty of evidence of the Romans' road building skills in the well-preserved roads that criss-crossed the Welsh countryside. They established a network of roads that were built well enough to survive centuries of Welsh weather! Some of the best stretches of Roman highway to see is the 260 km (160-mile) route known collectively as 'Sarn Helen' which connects Aberconwy in the north and Carmarthen in the west.

Other Roman roads include the Fosse Way and Watling Street which both connected strategic points for ease of both trade and communication. Today, some of the Roman routes are still the major transportation routes in Wales.

Roman forts and settlements also dotted the Welsh landscape and these settlements not only contributed to the Romanisation of the local population, but also left a lasting architectural legacy that is still visible in the ruins scattered across Wales.

- Parts of Y Gaer- the largest Roman fort can still be seen standing beside the River Usk near Brecon.
- Overlooking the famous castle of Caernarfon stands the Roman fort of Segontium, which was used by the Romans for most of their occupation.
- The skill of the Roman engineers can be admired at Dolaucothi in Pumsaint, which is the only Roman gold mine in Britain and has an elaborate series of aqueducts.

(Roman Wales | Cadw, n.d.)

The influence of Latin

Latin, the language of the Romans, also left its mark on Welsh vocabulary and elements of it can still be found in the Welsh language today. Additionally, the introduction of Christianity by the Romans significantly shaped the religious landscape of Wales. The establishment of churches and the spread of Christian teachings had a profound and lasting impact on the spiritual life of the Welsh people.

The legacy of Roman law

Roman law and governance systems also

played a crucial role in shaping the political structure of Wales. The Romans introduced a centralised administration, with local officials responsible for implementing Roman laws and policies. This administrative framework laid the foundation for future governance structures in Wales and influenced the development of Welsh legal and political institutions.

Post-Roman Wales

When the Roman army left Wales in the early 5th century, they left a vacuum as the country had been part of the Roman Empire for 300 years. It was a difficult time because there was no way life could return to pre-Roman times and many  of the Welsh communities had become dependent on the Roman Empire. Many historians feel that both England and Wales entered a 'Dark Ages', although this period is usually referred to as' 'Early Medieval".

The first legions had started to leave Wales in about AD 410 and within 100 years, they had all left to focus on other parts of the diminishing Roman Empire. Once the Romans had departed, Britain became divided into numerous small kingdoms. Wales became much more isolated than it had been and a decentralised society emerged. Wales was divided into the kingdoms of Brycheiniog, Dyfed, Gwent, Gwynedd, Morgannwg, Powys and Seisyllwg. The kingdoms had changing borders and lacked central authority. The strong Welsh identity did begin to take shape during this period, as the different communities developed a sense of shared culture, language, and identity.

The economy of Wales slumps

The economy of post-Roman Wales was based on subsistence farming and animal husbandry. Everyone was as self-sufficient as possible and became focused on meeting their basic needs within their community. Trade and commerce which had thrived under the Romans quickly declined. In the years that followed, the Roman infrastructure including the roads and villas fell into disrepair.

During the years 800- 900, the Welsh princes tried unsuccessfully to unite the different Welsh kingdoms, but usually ended up fighting each other. The princes were also faced with many invasions by outsiders - the Irish to the west and the Anglo-Saxons to the east. There were many conflicts over land and natural resources and these conflicts helped to define the borders of the Welsh kingdoms.

Christianity flourishes...

There was a spread of Christianity in post-Roman Wales, with the conversion of the people to Christianity steadily developing. Missionaries from Ireland and the Roman Church helped to spread the Christian faith and also established monastic communities which became great centres of learning. Britain's oldest religious school was founded in Llantwit Major and was where several Welsh saints studied. The first church was built on the site where Llandaff Cathedral stands today. As the years passed, the Welsh Church developed with its own characteristics and traditions that were quite different from the Roman Church.

An exciting current archaeological excavation....

There is currently a great deal of excitement amongst archaeologists in Wales. For the last two years they have been excavating an early mediaeval burial ground they uncovered within the grounds of Fonmon Castle near Cardiff. The graveyard dates from the 6th or 7th century and comprises about 70 graves, 18 of these have already been excavated. The site has caused interest as the excavated graves contain well-preserved skeletons, many of them placed in unconventional positions and buried with unusual artefacts including pottery, animal bones and a small carved wooden peg - probably from a game. Several imported items have also been found including fragments of glass from Bordeaux and pottery- thought to have come from North Africa.

Some skeletons are lying on their backs, but others are on their sides or even in a crouched position, with their knees drawn up to their chest. The skeletons have proved fascinating as several have front teeth that have been worn in an unusual manner - suggesting they were used like tools for a craft such as textile making or basketry.

Stability at last for post-Roman Wales

The 7th and 8th centuries saw much more stability in post-Roman Wales, as boundaries between kingdoms became well-defined and there was also a consolidation of power.

"In AD 757 - 796, the impressive linear earthwork called Offa's Dyke was built to help define the border between England and Wales – from a point near Prestatyn in the north, to Chepstow in the south. The dyke measured 82 km(132 miles) and was 20 metres(66 feet) in width." What Is the Offa's Dyke Path?, n.d.)

Peace would not last for long as the Viking raids in the 9th and 10th centuries posed new challenges. More defensive hill forts were quickly constructed as an increasing number of raids by the Vikings were made along the 600 miles of vulnerable Welsh coastline.

The impact of the Norman Conquest

During the 11th century, the Norman Conquest of England, brought new external pressures to Wales. The Norman lords were keen to expand into Welsh territories and this led to more conflict and the construction of many wooden motte-and-bailey castles for defence. The struggles between the Welsh rulers and the Normans was to continue for centuries, shaping the intricate relationships between the two societies.

CHAPTER 4
THE ARRIVAL OF THE NORMANS

In 1066, the Normans from France, successfully invaded England. During the following years 1067–1081, the Normans made several efforts at conquering Wales, but these were not undertaken with the same fervour and determination that the English invasion had been. Consequently, these first invasions failed. William the Conqueror had quickly strengthened his rule of the English kingdom and had established earldoms along the Welsh border. The Norman lords of these earldoms started to try expand their lands westwards into Wales.

In 1081, a much stronger Norman invasion of southern Wales was led by William who created a new defence point at Cardiff. During the following years, there were numerous forays by the Normans into Wales and they successfully captured and settled in the Vale of Glamorgan in the south of the country. They made Pembroke their new stronghold.

During his final years, William the Conqueror had difficulties, not only in his lands overseas, but with his son Robert and the Danes who repeatedly threatened to invade England. William died in September 1087, during a military campaign in northern France. Before his death, William the Conqueror ensured that his sons were given power. Robert was given Normandy and England was given to his second son - who was also called William. His youngest son, Henry was given a sizable amount of money. The king also left money to the church and the poor and instructed that all prisoners should be released.

The Domesday Book

This world famous manuscript records life in much of England and parts of Wales in the 11th century. It was completed in 1086 under the orders of William the Conqueror. The king decided that the survey was necessary as many of the Norman lords were arguing about land. He also felt that it was a good way to establish where the wealth of the country lay. He was personally running short of funds and establishing how much tax-money he could get from the land would be beneficial. The script was drawn up by six scribes and then checked by a seventh.

The Domesday book lists 13,000 places and many of them still survive today. There are details of which areas were woodland, meadow and pasture. The manuscript also reveals how many buildings had been destroyed during the Norman Invasion and Interestingly, how wealthy many of the 200 Norman lords had become.

The Domesday book can be viewed online:-

https://www.nationalarchives.gov.uk/help-with-your-research/research-guides/domesday-book/#:

(The National Archives, 2023)

12th century England and Wales

William II reigned in England until August 1100, when he was accidently killed whilst out hunting in the New Forest. The crown of England passed to his younger brother Henry, who was crowned Henry I in August 1100.

Henry was keen to establish a large Norman settlement in South Wales and ordered the construction of a royal castle at Carmarthen in 1109. The Welsh princes however, were far from happy and refused to swear loyalty to the new king. Instead, they took every opportunity to take land back from the Normans, whenever they could.

Although Wales was never totally invaded by the Normans, they did firmly establish themselves in South Wales. Norman rule in England between the years 1066-1154, had a big impact on Wales – although the impact varied from one region to another - just as the allegiance of the Welsh to the Norman kings  varied. In 1114, Henry I invaded Gwynedd and Gruffardap Cynan and the King of Gwynedd was defeated and forced to pay homage to Henry. In complete contrast, the following year, Henry knighted Owain ap Cadwgan for his honourable services to the crown in Normandy. In 1116 there was another Welsh revolt led by Gruffydd who took Swansea, Carmarthen and Kidwelly castles - but failed to take Aberystwyth.

These troubles amongst the Welsh continued throughout the Norman rule of England, Wales remained divided into a number of small independent kingdoms – with some Norman lords (known as Marcher Lords) successfully expanding their territories into Wales. By building castles, the Marcher Lords were able to effectively control the English/ Welsh border.

Henry I died in December 1135 and was succeeded by his nephew, Stephen (1096 – 1154). Henry I had reared Stephen who had pledged to support Henry's daughter Matilda to become Queen. Many of the English nobles did want to be ruled by a woman and she was also resented by the Normans for marrying into the royal Angevin family. Consequently, when the king's death was declared, Stephen hurried across the Channel to claim the crown.

Stephen was a pleasant and jovial king but ineffective. He dragged England through years of civil war as he fought his rival, Matilda, for the crown. Stephen had originally had the support of the church but lost this when he arrested the powerful Bishop of Salisbury. Matilda with the support of her half-brother, Robert the Earl of Gloucester, decided to seize the opportunity to invade England. Matilda did well and brought much of the west of England under her control. Stephen gradually regained control and in 1148, Matilda, fled England.

In his final years, Stephen was happy just to do his best to protect the throne so he could pass it on to his son, Eustace. In January 1153, Henry of Anjou who was Matilda's son, invaded England to claim the throne. That summer, Eustace died and Stephen was devastated. He happily signed the

Treaty of Wallingford stating that Henry would be his successor. Throughout his reign, Wales had remained an unsettled country in which he had had little interest.

Stephen I was the last Norman king and when he died, one year after signing the treaty, Henry was crowned Henry II of England.

Emergence of the Welsh princes

The Welsh princes began to rise to power during the early Middle Ages, particularly in the 9th and 10th centuries. This period saw the emergence of regional leaders who asserted authority over various territories in Wales. However, it was during the 11th and 12th centuries that Welsh princes like Gruffydd ap Llywelyn and Owain Gwynedd significantly expanded their influence and consolidated their power. They engaged in both internal conflicts with other Welsh rulers and external struggles against the invading Anglo-Normans. This period of Welsh history witnessed the formation of principalities and the assertion of Welsh autonomy before eventual integration into the kingdom of England.

During the 12th century, the Welsh princes like Owain Gwynedd and his successors spent much of their time opposing numerous attempts to seize power and land made by the Normans.

Through military resistance and a number of strategic alliances, the princes managed to remain united – although there were occasions when they had conflicts amongst themselves as they vied for supremacy.

The Norman legacy

- Norman architecture has a distinctive style, the structures were large and built in stone and incorporated a variety of architectural elements. The Normans were equally artistic with metal and stone.
- Norman castles were impressive with a square keep, moats and drawbridges. The Normans built more castles across Europe than any other power.
- Chepstow Castle was one of the first Norman castles built in Wales and lies on

the border between England and Wales.
- The Normans wore simple clothing but their style became more elaborate as they became wealthy.

(Historian, 2023)

Everyday life in Wales in Norman times

The influence of the Normans on the Welsh varied in the different regions. There were areas where there was interaction between the two and this to both an exchange of cultural ideas and adaption of ways. In the border areas, controlled by the Marcher Lords, a very distinctive culture emerged which was a blend of Welsh and Norman influences and traditions. Nevertheless, Wales managed to retain its individual identity and this would lead to further conflict in the future..

Throughout Norman rule the Welsh maintained their own legal and social systems. Welsh laws were known as 'Cyfraith Hywel' and were used for many aspects of everyday life. Welsh society was based on the system of tribal territories known as 'cantrefs' and 'commotes' and this practice continued.

Welsh remained the dominant language and continued to thrive and cultural heritage was enriched by a number of excellent Welsh poets and historians.

The emergence of the Welsh principalities

The Normans arrived in Wales, just one year after the Norman Conquest of England. Powerful Norman lords established themselves along the border between England and Wales and regularly made forays into Wales. The Normans established border strongholds at Chester, Shrewsbury and Hereford

William the Conqueror was keen to extend his power over Wales and captured the fertile valleys and lowlands but found much of the country had rugged terrain and was met by the fierce resistance of the Welsh. The land along the border became known as 'The Marches' and the Norman 'Marcher Lords' did their utmost to impose their rule on the Welsh lords – but were met with great resistance.

A number of Welsh principalities had evolved prior to the Norman invasion and these were strengthened. The Welsh princes fortified their strongholds and often played rival Norman lords against each other- which was easy to do as there were many divisions amongst the Normans. The conflict was not just military but also cultural and social. A new class of Anglo- Welsh landowner appeared too. These were Welshmen who had served the Normans and were given land as a reward for their military service.

Although there were huge cultural differences,  there was some cultural exchange between the Normans and Welsh- some of the Welsh princes adopted Norman customs and some Norman lords married wealthy Welsh ladies. Wales continued to be a patchwork of principalities for generations to come and the struggle for control continued well beyond the mediaeval period.

CHAPTER 5
MEDIEVAL WALES

The Plantagenet dynasty ruled mediaeval England from 1154 to 1485. There were 14 Plantagenet kings- beginning with Henry II (1154-1189) and ending with Richard III (1452-1485). The relationship between the Plantagenet kings and Wales was a complex one and shaped by military conflicts, political alliances, and attempts to integrate Wales into the English administrative and legal system. The conquest and subsequent governance of Wales had long-lasting effects on the history and identity of the country.

The House of Plantagenet is actually an 'umbrella term' coined by modern historians that covers four different royal houses from the Angevins (who were also Counts of Anjou) the main family of Plantagenet after they had loss their French lands, followed by the rival Houses of Lancaster and York – whose rivalry culminated in the War of the Roses.

The Plantagenet kings had varying degrees of involvement in Wales. Here is a brief overview of those Plantagenet kings who did have key relationships with Wales.

Wales in the 12th Century

Henry II (1154–1189)

Henry II's reign marked the beginning of the Plantagenet dynasty. He was one of the kings who was actively involved in Welsh affairs-particularly in asserting English authority over the region. Henry sought to expand his control in Wales, using both military force and diplomatic means. He initiated the construction of castles, such as those at Rhuddlan and Aberystwyth, as a way of consolidating English influence.

Richard I (1189–1199)

Better known as Richard the Lionheart and famous for his involvement in the Crusades, Richard I had limited direct engagement with Wales during his short reign. His focus was more on foreign affairs and his military campaigns in the Holy Land.

John (1199–1216)

King John faced many challenges in Wales, dealing with conflicts and power struggles among the Welsh princes. He attempted to exert control through alliances and military campaigns. The signing of the Magna Carta in 1215 (though not directly related to Wales) had broader implications for governance and law in Wales.

The Magna Carta (1215)

The Magna Carta, meaning "The Great Charter", was signed at Runnymede on June 15, 1215, by King John to deal with the grievances of the Welsh and Scottish rulers. Their main grievance was that John had more power over both countries than any English king before him. A good example of this was when in 1211 the king forced Llywelyn Farr - who was Prince of North Wales - to surrender a large area of land and give King John hostages- including Farr's own son Gruffyd- as security. The Magna Carta was a very important document as it established the principles of limited government and the rule of law. The charter asserted the rights of the barons against the arbitrary actions of the king. Some historians describe it as setting the foundations for the development of constitutional government.

Although the Magna Carta was primarily aimed at settling the grievances of the English barons, its principles were far-reaching and it affected the governance and rights of the Welsh. Later versions of the  Magna Carta included points specifically concerning Welsh law and governance.

'In chapter 56 of Magna Carta, John promised that, if had dispossessed Welshmen of their lands and liberties in England or Wales without lawful judgement of their peers—their social equals—they would be immediately restored. Any dispute was to be settled by judgement of peers.

In chapter 57, John promised to return Gruffydd immediately to Llywelyn, and also to restore all the hostages of Wales and the charters that he had extracted as security for "peace", which meant for "good"—or, as the Welsh would have thought it, "servile"— behaviour.

https://www.parliament.uk/about/living-heritage/evolutionofparliament/2015-parliament-in-the-making/2015-historic-anniversaries/magna-carta/magna-carta---

wales-scotland-and-ireland/

Wales in the 13ᵗʰ century

Henry III (1216–1272)

Henry III's reign saw continued efforts to establish English dominance in Wales. Henry faced resistance from Welsh leaders like Llywelyn the Great. The Treaty of Montgomery in 1267 recognised Llywelyn's authority over parts of Wales, though he still owed homage to the English crown.

Edward I (1272–1307)

Edward I's rule had a significant impact on Wales. Edward's attempts to conquer Wales included the construction of the famous "Iron Ring" of castles. The castles were built in the late 13ᵗʰ and early 14ᵗʰ century to consolidate English control over Wales. The castles built include Conwy, Harlech, Caernarfon and Beaumaris. All the castles were built in carefully chosen strategic positions to suppress any Welsh uprisings. All the castles were formidable military structures which doubled as administrative centres. With their construction, Edward I was showing his determination to assert his authority over the Welsh.

Following the deaths of the powerful Welsh leaders Llewelyn and Dafydd of Gwynedd,

Edward thought that to take total control of Wales would be easy, but he was wrong as there were a series of revolts. This meant that Edward had to spend much time in Wales, before finally being successful in seizing a large portion of the country.

The importance of the Statute of Rhuddlan (1284)

The Statute of Rhuddlan in 1284 was an important document as it formally annexed Wales to the English Crown-

"One of the tools Edward used to effect this change was the Statute of Rhuddlan (later, and erroneously called the Statute of Wales). According to this statute, the counties of Anglesey, Meirionnydd, and Caernarfon were created out of the remnants of Llewelyn's Gwynedd, and staffed with sheriffs to collect taxes and administer justice.

The Statute of Rhuddlan helped define the roles of these officials and the means by which they were to enforce this essentially foreign system of law within the areas of English influence in Wales." (Britain Express, n.d.-b)

The Welsh princes during the 13th centur

The 13th century was a difficult time for the

Welsh princes as it was marked by the increasing encroachment on their lands by the English – especially during the reign of Edward I. The stronger Welsh princes - such as Llywelyn the Great- resisted English domination, but in the years 1282- 1283, Edward I was finally successful and Welsh lands were brought under the English crown.

The first Prince of Wales - 1301

The title 'Prince of Wales' was created in 1301 by King Edward I and was bestowed on his son, Edward, who later became Edward II. The duties of the role have evolved through the centuries. The title is always given to the monarch's eldest son who is the heir apparent. His role as Prince of Wales helps him to prepare him for his future role as monarch as he must meet government officials and fully understand how the government works. The title is not automatic and must be bestowed by the monarch on their son.

Wales in the 14th century

Edward II (1307–1327)

Edward II faced internal strife and challenges to his rule - including discontent in Wales. His inability to effectively govern contributed to great unrest, and during his reign, there were notable uprisings in Wales, led by figures like Llywelyn Bren and later, Owain Glyndŵr. There would be further rebellions led by Owain Glyndŵr in Henry IV's reign (1399-1413) and these rebellions would have a lasting impact on the difficult relationship between England and Wales.

The Black Death (1348- 1350)

In the mid-14th century, the plague swept across Wales and was at its worst between 1348-1350. Also known as '*The Black Death*', the plague was a deadly pandemic that was spread by close contact with infected people and contaminated goods. The plague brought widespread death to Wales and this resulted in an economic upheaval that had repercussions for generations afterwards.

The symptoms of the plague were horrible with high fever, vomiting and darkened patches of skin caused by internal bleeding. Death was swift and the mortality rate was 80% in some parts of Wales. The plague affected everyone – whatever their age, social class or background and it brought with it fear and paranoia. There were food shortages, and no medicine. Trade routes were disrupted and the high death rate led to labour shortages too.

The impact on Wales was immense as entire families were wiped out, communities were shattered and a wealth of skills and talents were lost, as well as labourers and artisans and this all led to a rise in prices.

The Welsh princes during the 14th century

The Welsh were still keen to be independent and this led to regular uprisings – including those led by Owain Glyndŵr. He briefly established a Welsh parliament and gained strong support both from the Welsh nobles and a number of English rebels. The revolt did eventually fail and Wales remained under English control

Owain Glyndŵr (1359- ?1415)

Owain Glyndŵr was a nobleman who was

descended from the Princes of Powys and claimed the title Prince of Wales. To many, he is a national hero. Like many, he was furious with the English, the seizure of Welsh lands and increasingly heavy taxes. In 1400, he began a revolt which proved surprisingly successful as he managed to unite various Welsh factions and win numerous battles against English soldiers. His soldiers controlled several significant parts of Wales – including the capital, Cardiff.

In 1404 he established a Welsh Parliament and was crowned Prince of Wales, which strengthened the Welsh identity. Despite these early victories, the rebellion began to falter as he received little external support and  there was infighting amongst his followers. The last mention of Glyndŵr was made in historical records dated 1412. The exact date of his death remains unknown. His rebellion left a lasting legacy for Welsh cultural identity and he remains a popular character in Welsh folklore and history and is celebrated for his defiance against English domination.

Owain Glyndŵr. (n.d.). Medieval Wales.

Retrieved from https://owain-glyndwr.wales/age_of_the_princes/mediaeval_wales_detail.html

(*Wales in the Middle Ages*, n.d.)

Wales in the 15ᵗʰ century

Henry VI (1422–1461 and 1470–1471)

Henry VI was a weak king with poor leadership skills which led to political instability that was marked by the Wars of the Roses. These were a series of dynastic conflicts within the Plantagenet family.

The instability the conflicts caused was far reaching and indirectly affected Wales. Many of the Welsh nobility aligned themselves with either one side or the other, leading to a number of internal conflicts in Wales too. The authority of the English monarchy was greatly weakened too and Welsh leaders like Owain Glyndŵr took advantage of this to launch further uprisings against English rule in Wales. The Marcher Lords gained autonomy and power and this too increased the complexity of the country's political landscape.

Some of the Battles of the Wars of the Roses spilled over the border into Wales as a number of military actions took place on the border. This added to the instability to the area.

Richard III (1483- 1485)

Richard was a very controversial king who many believe was involved in the disappearance of his two nephews - whose father, Edward IV had been king. The young princes each had a claim to the throne. The princes were referred to as 'The Princes in the Tower' and the elder, Edward, had already been proclaimed Edward V on the death of his father. Richard III declared that the boys' parents had not been legally married so the young Edward could not be the legitimate heir and thus claimed the throne for himself. The boys were last seen in public in June 1483 and were never seen or heard of again.

Richard's reign was brief as he was defeated and killed at the Battle of Bosworth and with him died the Plantagenet dynasty. Henry VII was the victor at Bosworth and brought the War of the Roses to an end. He was crowned King of England – and the first Tudor king.

Interesting facts about the Plantagenets

- The Plantagenet dynasty saw some of the most violent episodes in history, including the Hundred Years' War between England and France, the Peasants' Revolt and the War of the Roses. This was a civil war between the Houses of Lancaster and York and it brought an end to the dynasty.
- Drone warfare is thought of as a 21st century method, but it was first used in the 13th century between Henry III and Simon de Montfort! De Montfort planned to use cockerels with fire bombs attached to their feet to attack the capital, London. His ideas were flawed because cockerels can only fly a short

distance and their feathers are inflammable! (Jones, 2022)

- The name 'Plantagenet' was first used for Geoffrey V, the Count of Anjou who always wore a sprig from a broom plant (*planta genista*) in his hat. Richard Duke of York took the name in the 15th century.
- The Plantagenets lost the 100 Years War against France. The war was a series of conflicts between 1337-1453 and was waged over the succession to the throne of France. France defeated England and this led to civil war. (*10 Fast Facts About the Plantagenets*, n.d.)

Everyday life in Medieval Wales

Life during the Plantagenet dynasty was hard for both men and women. They lived a hand -to-mouth existence and the men often died in conflict and the women in childbirth. If they survived these, then illness and infection usually killed them. Few people lived beyond their mid-40s.

Life was focused on the village and the people worked hard, wore simple clothes and ate a meagre diet. Whilst the English were farmers, the Welsh were more often herders unless they lived in the more fertile areas on the lowlands. There were fewer villages in Wales because of the challenging terrain. During 1100–1300, however, 80 towns were developed. This development was encouraged by the Welsh princes and the Marcher Lords as they would bring extra wealth. Trade in the towns also developed and the Welsh began trading animal skins and fleeces plus cheese in return for such commodities as iron, wheat and salt - but trade was often interrupted by conflict.

"There were three main social groups: the uchelwyr – the upper class, thebonheddwyr – the freemen and the taeogion – the unfree peasants. Each group had its role in society. (Sarah, 2017)

Culture in Wales

During the period 1100-1300, a group of Welsh poets known as the *Gogynfeirdd* received support from the Welsh kings and princes. One poem emerged as the best – *the Elergy of Gruffudd ab Yr Ynad Coch to Llewelyn ap Gruffudd.* Slowly as the number of princes diminished, the patronage of the poets was passed to the nobility. The poets themselves formed a society of verse called Dafydd ap Gwilym and a new style of poetry emerged rich in *cynghanedd* –which was the term given to an intricate pattern of chiming sounds.

The first Eisteddfod

Owain Gwynedd was a strong Welsh king who had built castles and defeated the English in 1136. He and his collaborator, Rhys ap Gruffudd held a magnificent music and poetry festival in Cardigan Castle in 1176 and this was regarded as the first *eisteddfod*. Traditional Welsh culture has been kept alive by these competitive music and poetry festivals which are today there are local and national events with the Royal National Eisteddfod  being the largest and held each August. Today this event also includes Welsh craftsmen. This event is held alternate years in North and South Wales.

Literature

The Mabinogion Collection is a collection of 11 stories that has been translated from Medieval Welsh manuscripts that tell tales of pre-Christian Celtic history, religion, mythology and traditions. The collection is considered to be the country's greatest contribution to European literature.

Song

Singing became a popular pastime and the natural ability of the Welsh to sing in perfect harmony soon became apparent and is a talent that has received worldwide acclaim over the centuries.

During this period, both wood carving and stone carving became highly developed – particularly in the 15th century – with the construction of castles, churches and monasteries. The parish church in Gresford is regarded as the finest example of the work of Welsh stone masons.

CHAPTER 6
WALES UNDER THE TUDORS

The Tudor kings and queens are among the most recognised of English monarchs, Richard Rex on the website https://www.historic-uk.com/HistoryUK/HistoryofEngland/The-Tudors/ suggests that they had iconic status because -

"The age of print and Renaissance portraiture gave them huge advantages over the kings of earlier centuries, but they were the first English monarchs to take such pains over their public image, and it is a tribute to the success of the Tudor image-makers."

The Tudor monarchy lasted for 118 years from 1485- 1603 and comprised of five kings and queens who were of English/ Welsh descent from the Tudors of Penmynydd (Tuduriaid Penmynydd) and Catherine of Valois. They ruled the kingdom of England, Wales and the Lordship of Ireland.

Henry VII (1485-1509)

Harri's famous victory in the Wars of the Roses at the Battle of Bosworth saw the defeat of Richard and Harri becoming King Henry VII. The House of Lancaster had triumphed over the House of York. But to Welsh men and women, the victory was entirely theirs.

"Harri was the genuine article, born in Wales. He was conscious of his roots, enjoying the things the Welsh are famous for – music, poetry, literature and sport. He flew the Welsh flag, appointed Welshmen to influential government and religious posts, and returned to Wales a certain status and self-confidence that had been shattered by previous events.

(The Tudors in Wales | Cadw, n.d.)

Henry was a Welshman as his grandfather was Owen Tudor, a Welsh courtier from Anglesey and the second husband of Catherine of Valois. She had previously been married to Henry V and was mother to Henry VI. When she married Owen Tudor, they had several children including Edmund Tudor- Henry's father.

As a symbolic gesture, when he was crowned

king, Henry (who was a Lancaster) married Elizabeth of York - thus uniting the two warring houses and bringing stability to England. During his reign he worked hard to strengthen royal power and to bring Wales under English control.

Henry reignited the desire to build castles which had not been seen since the reign of Edward I. Many castles were transformed from solid military strongholds into more comfortable defences modelled on the latest French designs. A good example of this is Raglan and the Octagonal tower built at Cardiff Castle. Tretower in the Brecon Beacons (Bannau Brycheiniog) is well worth seeing as it successfully combines a strong mediaeval style with a late mediaeval courthouse.

The Welsh princes in the 15th century

During the 15th century, England still dominated Wales. There was unrest and occasional rebellions. One of the key figures during the late 15th and early 16th centuries was Rhys ap Thomas who was a powerful Welsh nobleman rather than prince who was born into the House of Dinefwr in 1449.

In 1485, Henry Tudor landed in Wales to

challenge the usurper, Richard III. Rhys ap Thomas, pledged allegiance to Henry and provided him with crucial military support. At the Battle of Bosworth, Rhys ap Thomas led a strong contingent of Welsh forces and helped Henry to secure victory over Richard III and the crown of England. Local legend tells how it was Rhys ap Thomas who fatally wounded Richard. As his reward, Henry bestowed titles on him including Deputy Constable of Carmarthen Castle. Rhys ap Thomas became one of the most influential figures in Wales. He continued to support Henry and his successors. His support for the Tudor dynasty helped stabilise Wales.

Rhys ap Thomas died in 1525, leaving a lasting impact on Welsh politics.

Wales in the 16th century

Henry VIII (1509-1547)

Without a doubt, Henry VIII is the most famous of the Tudor kings - best known for his six wives and the English Reformation. Henry liked Wales, but not to the same degree as his father.

In 1536, the Act of Union was passed and this abolished the independent rule of Wales and incorporated Wales into the Kingdom of England. Henry did this because he feared a sea invasion on the Welsh coast - either by France or Spain.

When Henry died in 1547, the crown was passed to his nine year old son, Edward VI, so England was ruled by his 'Royal Advisors'. There was a concerted effort to impose Protestantism – which had been introduced by the Reformation – on the Welsh.

Mary I (1553-1558)

Mary was Henry VIII's daughter who attempted to restore Catholicism to England and Wales, and this led to great religious persecution in Wales.

Elizabeth I (1558-1603)

Elizabeth was Mary's half sister and ruled England for more than 44 years. She continued to try and fully integrate the government of Wales with England, but she was keen to maintain a stability in Wales too, so the Welsh identity and culture was allowed to thrive. However, by the time of her death in 1603 England was on the brink of civil war again and many Welsh castles would be damaged.

Interesting facts about the Tudors

- In Tudor times, people were very superstitious and also believed in magic. Some people wore an amulet such as a precious stone or piece of coloured cloth to protect them against disease. Others carried parts of an animal for good luck– with a rabbit's foot being particularly popular.

- The Tudors enjoyed playing board games and backgammon, chess, and card games all became popular.

- The wealthy enjoyed all kinds of exotic meat including badgers, otters, tortoises and dolphins.

- Tudor medicines were based on ideas from the Ancient Greek doctor, Hippocrates. Ordinary people could not afford a doctor so would be given herbal remedies by the 'wise woman' in their community.

- One of the largest and heaviest cannons used by soldiers in Tudor times was the Mons Meg. This cannon could fire a cannon ball a distance of just under two miles (3 km) and today is displayed at Edinburgh Castle.

Everyday life in Wales under the Tudors

Life was difficult and many more people did not live more than 35 -40 years. Water was often the source of infection as it was collected from steams or pumps and was often dirty – and infected by raw sewage. Meals usually consisted of a vegetable broth and a hard grey bread made from either rye or barley. If they were lucky, some communities with animals had cheese, milk and eggs. In complete contrast, the rich Welsh princes had opulent and elegant clothes and enjoyed expensive foods including veal and venison and often French wines too. The rich enjoyed hunting, falconry and jousting. Such games as tennis and bowls also made an appearance. In sharp contrast, poor people played football – but were only allowed to do so once a year, on Christmas Day.

The Tudor Legacy for Wales

The pivotal point for Wales in Tudor times was the Act of Union in 1536. Many historians argue that the union was not between England and the country of Wales, but between England and the March area of southern Wales. The Act was passed solely by the English Parliament, with no Welsh present. Dr John Davies is convinced though that the Act of Union was good for Wales -

It was the events of the Tudor reign that ensured that the subsequent history of Wales was a happier story than was the subsequent history of Ireland. The 'Act of Union', although it can be seen as an arbitrary act of annexation, brought about a single citizenship in Wales, a boon of immense significance. (BBC - History - Wales Under the Tudors, 2011)

CHAPTER 7
WALES IN THE 17TH CENTURY

For Wales, the Stuart period (1603- 1714) was a period of political, social, and cultural changes. These changes were closely related to the developments taking place in Britain as a whole. Wales was now incorporated into the Kingdom of England and the Welsh princes no longer had any significant power. The two Acts of Union (1536 and 1543) completed both the legal and administrative integration of Wales into the Kingdom of England. The remnants of self-government in Wales went and English law and administration was adopted throughout the country. The four Stuart kings and one queen all had difficult reigns.

James I (1603- 1625)

The reign of the Stuarts begins with the union of the crowns of Scotland and England.

James VI of Scotland had been king for 36 years, when he became James I of England following the death of Queen Elizabeth I. Politically, the countries remained independent but for the first time, the King was King of the United Kingdom.

The reign of James I was a complex time for the Welsh as he was trying to consolidate English control over Wales and he was trying to make the Welsh more English by promoting the use of English language and law and appointing English officials to all the key positions in the Welsh administration. The Welsh strongly resisted much of what James sought to achieve and worked hard to preserve their language, culture and autonomy.

Despite these tensions, there were some positive developments for Wales including modernisation of its administration and legal systems as well as advancements in education and literature.

King James was a keen theologian and during his reign ordered a new translation of the Bible. He was a tolerant man but after the Gunpowder Plot of 1605 by the Roman Catholic Guy Fawkes and his accomplices to blow up the Houses of Parliament, James introduced stiff penalties for Roman Catholics. The end of his reign was marked by financial pressures caused by the Thirty Years War in Europe and impending war with Spain.

Charles I 1625-1649

Charles I's reign was a tumultuous period in British history. His reign was marked by political strife, religious tensions, and civil war. He tried to exert control over Wales- both politically and economically- and this was met with sharp resistance by the Welsh nobles. There was great discontent amongst ordinary Welsh people too, when he imposed greater taxation and changes to land tenure.

There was religious tension between Charles and the nonconformist groups in Wales including the Calvinistic Methodists - led by preacher Vavasor Powell (1617-1670). The tensions were sparked when Charles tried to impose the Anglican liturgy on them. Powell was a key figure in the spread of dissenting religious movements in Wales. During his reign, Wales enjoyed economic growth as the country's ironworks and coal mines flourished – particularly in the south. Charles brought in new trade and taxation policies which negatively impacted Welsh merchants and landowners, causing more unrest.

Charles' reign culminated in the English Civil War (1642-1651) and this brought military campaigns and economic disruption to Wales – as well as divided loyalties to the Welsh. The Welsh found themselves fighting on both sides of the conflict. Sir Thomas Myddleton, a notable Welsh nobleman for example, supported Parliamentarians, led by Oliver Cromwell.

Civil War and Interregnum 1642-1660

The Interregnum was the period between the execution of Charles I in 1649 and the restoration of the monarchy in 1660. This period is also referred to as the 'Commonwealth Period'.

Following the Civil War between the Royalists (Cavaliers) and the Parliamentarians (also known as Roundheads) under Oliver Cromwell – known as the Lord Protector- the monarchy was abolished and the Commonwealth established under the leadership of Oliver the  Cromwell. It was a republican-style government which had power- as did the military. This was a period of great unrest with Cromwell's forces engaged in military campaigns in Scotland and Ireland as well as several domestic revolts.

Cromwell died in 1658 and his son, Richard, briefly became Lord Protector, but lacked his father's political acumen which led to the collapse of the Protectorate and the restoration of the monarchy.

Oliver Cromwell is one of the most important men in England's history, but everything he struggled for collapsed within two decades of his death. The army, Parliament and the citizens of London grappled with each other for control of the country, and even the army no longer remained a united political force.

- Charles River Editors, taken from The Stuart Restoration, The History and Legacy of the English Monarchy's Return to Power in the Late 17th Century

Charles II (1660-1685)

Charles II was in exile when he was invited back by Parliament to be crowned. His reign brought some stability, but its most notable events were probably the Great Plague of 1665, followed by the Fire of London in 1666. The King did achieve some developments for Wales even though his primary focus was on re-establishing the monarchy and consolidating his power. He supported the development of trade and industry in Wales and the ironworks and coal mines in the south thrived once again.

Charles also granted charters to some towns in Wales to promote trade and he made efforts to improve the transport infrastructure and communication between Wales and England. He also proposed plans for a university and other educational establishments in Wales although these would not come to fruition until the 19th century.

Anne (1702- 1714)

After the troubled reign of James II (1685-1689) and the joint reign of William and Mary, Anne came to the throne as the last Stuart monarch in 1702.There had been no interaction with Wales for years as in fact none of these monarchs had visited Wales!

Queen Anne, the last monarch of the Stuart dynasty. She reigned from 1702 to 1714. Her reign was marked by significant political, military, and social developments. The War of the Spanish Succession (1701-1714) had begun the year before she was crowned and would continue throughout her reign. England played a key role and because of this, Wales was involved too.

The Acts of Union in 1707 united England and Scotland to form the Kingdom of Great Britain. Wales had already legally integrated with England by the Acts of 1535 and 1542, the

Acts of Union did solidify both the political and constitutional status of Wales within the newly formed kingdom.

Anne's reign also saw the development of cultural and intellectual movements, and this had an impact on the cultural landscape of Wales.

Everyday life in Wales under the Stuarts

Many people still lived in the countryside in Stuart times, although many more had moved to the towns, where they lived in crowded conditions. In the beginning, many families had a hand-to-mouth existence but by the beginning of the 18th century, things were easier and families were living more comfortably than they had ever done. Life expectancy was still much shorter than it is today and 10- 25 women in every 100 died in childbirth. There was a clear distinction between male and female roles. Farming remained important to Wales and crops were still grown in the fertile Welsh valleys and animal husbandry continued where the soil was not so good and the terrain was more challenging. South Wales was more prosperous than the other regions in Wales because of the development of coal mining and the iron works.

For further reading about life in Stuart times https://www.historyextra.com/period/stuart/s tuart-britain-what-was-life-like-for-ordinary-people/

(Evans, 2022)

The Stuart legacy for Wales

The legacy that the Stuart dynasty left in Wales was multi-faceted and changed different aspects of Welsh life. Importantly, the Acts of Union integrated Wales much more fully into the Kingdom of England and had established English law in Wales.

This was a very unsettled period with numerous military conflicts for the English and the Welsh were often drawn into them. Like in the English Civil War, the Welsh often found themselves fighting on opposing sides.

There were significant changes to land ownership in Wales and many small estates were consolidated into much larger estates – displacing many small farmers. This brought changes to both the Welsh landscape and society.

There were also significant changes in religion in Wales - both during the English Civil War and the years of Interregnum. These changes saw a rise in Puritanism and dissenting religious movements and this had led to religious persecution and the suppression of Catholicism. The Stuarts also contributed to Welsh culture as they ardently supported the arts and literature, and this saw the emergence of many fine Welsh poets and writers.

Welsh culture in 17- 18th century

The biggest changes to the literary culture of Wales was the arrival of the Renaissance in Wales, followed by the printing press. In the 17th century the English government tried to suppress Welsh poems and books. Poets and writers were horrified as they wanted to preserve the Welsh language for future generations and many poems and books were written. There was a strong movement to ensure that Welsh was always spoken and written in church.

Poems were still written in strict metre and the anglesey poet, goronwy owen, was keen to preserve this style of poetry. The number of traditional musicians declined during this period and it became usual for singing to be accompanied by the harp – this was the beginning of choral music. During this period there was little development in the world of welsh art or sculpture.

CHAPTER 8

18TH CENTURY WALES AND THE HOUSE OF HANOVER

The House of Hanover comprised six monarchs. Finding the correct person to be king was difficult as two descendents of James II threatened to seize the crown in 1715 and 1746 and were supported by the Jacobites – this term comes from Jacobus, the Latin name meaning 'James'. The Hanoverian years of rule did stabilise and most of the monarchs reigned for many years.

George I (1714– 27)

George I was 52nd in line to the throne of England but was the closest Protestant – as required by the Act of Settlement. George was still not the ideal choice of monarch as he did not speak English and communicated with his ministers in French. He was 54 years old - when he was crowned which also made him the oldest monarch. He spent his time stabilising England after the tumultuous Stuart period. He did not undertake any special initiatives for Wales, but he did oversee the early stages of the Industrial Revolution which brought many economic changes to Wales. In 1721, Robert Walpole became England's first Prime Minister.

George III (1760–1820)

Like his grandfather George II, whom he succeeded in 1720, the reign of George III was a period of significant change – but he did not achieve anything specific for Wales, but the changes he made did impact Wales. The 18th century had seen the beginning of the Industrial Revolution which continued through the reign of George III. The expansion of many industries including coal mining and ironworks transformed both the Welsh economy and its landscape. The steel industry would follow later. George III improved the infrastructure with new roads, railways and later trains to ensure that the coal and iron from Wales could be easily transported to other parts of Britain.

Towards the end of the 18th century, there was what many describe as a 'Welsh Renaissance' with a great revival of Welsh Culture and language. Many great literary works were published at this time and the Gwyneddigion Society was founded. This all contributed to a strengthening of the feeling of Welsh identity.

Welsh soldiers in conflict overseas

There were a number of military conflicts during George III's reign including the Napoleonic Wars and American Revolutionary War and several Welsh regiments fought with distinction in these conflicts.

Although George III did not have any specific policies for Wales, the many developments of industry, culture and transport, benefited the country tremendously.

The early 19th century in Wales and industrialisation

The reigns of the last two Hanoverian kings – George IV (1820-1830) and William IV – did not have any significant impact on Wales, but nevertheless the country saw continual development.

George IV loved buildings and architecture and instructed several impressive buildings to be constructed. There were ongoing discussions in Parliament about Welsh identity and autonomy and there was an increased interest in Welsh affairs. There was further expansion of the Welsh industries, and this saw both urbanisation and population growth in the valleys of South Wales.

William IV was keen to reform the electoral system in Britain and in 1832, the Reform Act was passed. Whilst the act focused on England and Scotland, as the redistribution of parliamentary seats was part of the act, it ensured that Wales was still represented, which was important. There were also debates and reforms about the Church of England and

these had implications for Wales where the Church of England was firmly established. The Ecclesiastical Duties and Revenues Act of 1836 was tabled to reform the allocation of church revenue and reduce inefficiencies within the church and this had direct repercussions on the Welsh.

During William's reign industrialisation in Wales continued as did an increasing awareness of Welsh identity and culture. This was fuelled by the Welsh literary revival and the activities of the various organisations that promote Welsh language and culture. This increased awareness gave many people a renewed sense of their Welsh identity.

CHAPTER 9
VICTORIAN TIMES IN WALES

During the long reign of Queen Victoria, there were significant changes and developments in Wales – just as there had been in the reigns of her predecessors. A number of key developments that took place during her reign did impact Wales.

The Industrial Revolution continues

The Industrial Revolution continued to shape Wales and new industries included steel production and slate quarrying. Wales was already well known for its coal production – especially in the valleys of South Wales. The new railways facilitated the transportation of coal and other goods – including agricultural products- and this boosted Welsh economic development.

The first mining in Wales was in Roman Times, but during the Industrial Revolution, coal mining in Wales increased dramatically and became the key industry in Wales and also for the whole of Great Britain. The coal industry was focused in the Rhondda Valley and the South Wales Valleys, but there was another coalfield in Northeast Wales. By the end of the 19th century, Barry was the largest exporting docks in the world – with Cardiff a close second. The oldest continually worked coalfield in the world was the Tower Colliery in the South Wales Valleys. Welsh coal was in high demand and commanded a good price as it was considered to be high quality coal that burned well.

There was often discontent amongst the coal workers who were unhappy with their long hours, poor working conditions and wages. There were a number of protests against employers including a large one at Merthyr in 1831. It was essential that working conditions changed – and especially child labour.

"On 4 August 1842, a law was passed that stopped women and children under ten years from working underground in mines in Britain. Before this law was passed, it was common for whole families to work together underground to earn enough money for the family to live on. "

(What Jobs Did Children Do Underground? • Coal Mining and the Victorians • MyLearning, n.d.)

Big social changes

The Victorian era also saw many social changes including improvements in health, housing and education. The Public Health Act (1848) and the Education Act (1870) were passed to address social issues and to improve the well-being of many – particularly those in poorer Welsh communities.

The Rebecca Riots (1839- 1843)

Primarily centred on the rural parts of Carmarthenshire, Cardiganshire and Pembrokeshire, the Rebecca Riots were a series of protests that had been sparked by the increasing toll charges on the roads at a time when there was great economic hardship. The riots were given the name 'Rebecca' because the rioters dressed as women to conceal their identities. Their actions reminded many of the biblical story of Rebecca by the well which is in Genesis Chapter 24. The rioters destroyed toll gates and fences so that everyone could use the roads freely. The riots were non-violent and the rioters avoided harming anyone.

The riots made a significant impact because

they highlighted social and economic inequalities and the need for reform. Eventually the tolls were removed on many of the roads in Wales and discussions began about grievances in the area. The Rebecca Riots are remembered as a symbol of the Welsh resistance to injustice.

The Welsh cultural revival

The Welsh Cultural Revival continued and several organisations including Cymdeithas y Cymreigyddion (The Society of Welshmen) and the National Eisteddfod of Wales were key in promoting Welsh identity and national pride. A real boost to the Welsh was the fact that Queen Victoria took a keen interest in Wales and Welsh events and she  regularly visited Wales. On one particular visit, she stayed at Penrhyn Castle, and this captured the public imagination and there was a surge in tourism to the area and pride amongst the Welsh. The Victorian era played a crucial role in shaping Wales and its people.

Everyday life in Wales in the 19th century

At the beginning of the 19th century there

was great social inequality in both England and Wales, but industrialisation brought great changes to all classes as wealth grew. The 'middle class' emerged with a huge demand for a variety of goods and services which had previously only been enjoyed by the rich. Labour was cheap, and by 1900 about one third of women aged between 15- 20 years were in service.

Changes for the poor

With their new found wealth, the middle classes bought fine clothes – purple was the exciting new colour for women's dresses. They also bought beautiful china, cutlery from Sheffield and glass from Liverpool for their homes. Importantly, these items were all made in the United Kingdom – which was good for trade.

There were still millions of poor people. They worked incredibly long hours in poor conditions in factories, mines and docks. During Queen Victoria's reign, things did change for them. Food became cheaper as imports grew. Such delights as bananas started appearing in the cities! The Factory Acts of the 1830s reduced the number of working hours and improved the working conditions for both adults and children.

A new style of housing

Cheap terraces of houses were built and these were cheaper to buy. Good examples that can be seen are the slate workers' terraced house in Bethesda in North Wales and the terrace houses overlooking the sea at Beaumaris. A Victorian terrace house in Buckley, Flintshire was voted 'Wales' Home of the Year in 2022 (https://www.dailypost. co.uk /news/north-wales-news/inside-special-victorian-terrace-named-24759756). As well as improved housing, many more people had access to clean water, drains and some homes had gas. The horrors of the early 19th century workhouses became distant memories.

Education becomes a top priority.

Education for all became more important and in 1880, it became compulsory for children to attend school until the age of ten. There were new 'board' schools and church schools established. Few children had been able to read at the beginning of the century, but by the end, almost all children were literate. Interestingly, Welsh children were not encouraged to speak Welsh and were punished if they did. Their punishment was to wear a piece of wood called a 'Welsh Not' around their neck for the rest of the day. For the first time, children and their childhood were valued. Queen Victoria and her husband, Albert had nine children and for many became 'the ideal family'.

Theatres and music halls became popular and more people enjoyed sports with the new sports of lawn tennis and croquet quickly becoming popular.

Welsh Arts in the 19th century

Until the middle of the 19th century, Welsh artists found it impossible to earn a living from the home market and many had to live away from their homeland. In 1854, an Act of Parliament was passed that would fund the creation of new art schools – which included the Cardiff School of Art, built in 1865. The Royal Cambrian Academy of Art was founded in 1881 by a group of 31 English and Welsh artists who were based in the Conwy Valley. Betws-y-Coed became a centre for art and became popular as rail travel made it easier for English artists to spend time there.

The Welsh artist, Christopher Williams (1873-1934) was born in Maesteg and was famous for his portraits and Welsh landscapes which can be seen in the Glynn Vivian Art Gallery in Swansea, Newport Museum and others. Frank Brangwyn (1867-1956) was an artist, watercolourist and printmaker. He produced more than 12,000 pieces of art during his lifetime and is best known for his brightly coloured murals with details of animals and plants. His 1890 canvas entitled 'Funeral at Sea' won a medal at the Paris Salon, the following year.

The Welsh sculptor Sir William Goscombe John (1860-1952) was born in Cardiff but split his time between the city and London. He became well known for his public memorials – especially his war memorials for the men lost in the Second Boer War and World War I.

Augustus John (1878- 1961)

Augustus John was born in Tenby in 1878 and lived much of his life in the town. He and his older sister developed a love of drawing from their mother. He studied at the Slade School of Fine Art in London where he developed his distinctive style, influenced by arts such as Van Gogh and Gauguin. His landscapes are very distinctive as he uses expansive brushstrokes and intense colours. He is well known for his portrait painting too, of politicians, writers and other artists. Augustus John had a flamboyant character and he was a central figure in the bohemian communities in the cities of London and Paris. He was a forerunner in the development of modern British art.

19th century Welsh writers and poets

The beauty of the Welsh landscape has long inspired many to reach for their pen and there were a number of prolific Welsh writers in the 19th century. Thomas Edwards (1759-1858) was born in Flintshire and wrote a book on Welsh Orthography and an English/ Welsh dictionary. Robert Williams (1830-1877) was a Welsh language poet who was born in Ty'n-yr-ardd near Llanrwst. He wrote his poems under the Bardic name of Trebor Mai.

Ann Harriet Hughes (1852-1910) was a popular Welsh language novelist who wrote under the pen name of Gwyneth Vaughan. One of her contemporaries was Rhoda Broughton (1840- 1920) who also wrote novels and short stories in the Welsh language but was side-lined by many critics as she had the reputation of being sensationalist.

Although he was a Welsh journalist, Sir Henry Morton Stanley (1841-1904) was also an explorer who became famous when he went to central Africa in search of David Livingstone. On finding him, Stanley is credited with the  famous line- 'Dr. Livingstone I presume?' although this is much debated!

Important 19th century Welsh inventions

Sir William Robert Grave

This Welsh lawyer and scientist invented the fuel cell in 1839. This was to be the foundation of the development of clean energy technology which is still being developed to this day.

Richard Trevithick

Although he was born in Cornwall, which had close cultural ties with Wales, Trevithick spent much time in Wales. It was in Wales that he developed high pressure steam engines which were successfully used for early locomotives and steam powered machinery.

David Edward Hughes

Hughes was a successful Welsh- American inventor who is best known for the world's first microphone which he invented in 1878. The microphone would be used in both telecommunications industry and to advance audio recording technology.

Griffith John Griffith

Griffith was the scientist who invented flexible and transparent film – an idea patented in 1889. His invention led to the development of photographic film used in cameras and films.

The emergence of the male Welsh voice choir....

During the 19th century, the exclusively male choirs were found in many Welsh chapels. Originally, the men sang hymns but as the choir's popularity developed, their repertoire was broadened to include both traditional and modern songs as well as ballads. Often the choirs sang with no musical accompaniment, but others were accompanied by a lyre, harp or fiddle.

.... And the Welsh love of rugby

In 1823, a great new game had found its way across the Welsh borders. Rugby had been invented at Rugby School in England. The game was an instant success with the Welsh and quickly became entwined in Welsh culture and identity.

Wales played a significant role in the development of the game. The first recorded game took place in 1875 with teams from Lampeter College and Llandovery College. Rugby became particularly popular – especially in the industrial south and it was closely associated with the working class communities.

In 1881, Wales played England in the first international rugby match at Blackheath in London. Wales won and the Welsh rugby tradition had been ignited. Over the years, Wales has produced many legendary players – especially in the 1970s, which was a golden era.

One of the most iconic moments for Welsh rugby was in 1905 when Wales defeated New Zealand – then known as the 'Original All Blacks' – in a thrilling match in Cardiff. This moment is still celebrated in Welsh history.

Today, rugby is ingrained in the Welsh culture and there is passionate support for the national team – and great rivalry whenever they play England or Scotland! The game fosters pride and camaraderie amongst the Welsh and holds a special place in their hearts. The Welsh national team continues to play at the highest level.

CHAPTER 10
WALES IN THE EARLY 20TH CENTURY

During the 20th century, Wales saw many changes in its political, social and cultural landscapes. There were differing relationships with the monarch as Wales was an integral part of the United Kingdom.

The early 20th century

The last year of Victoria's reign

Queen Victoria's reign was both long and settled and this brought stability to Wales. The Queen had a keen interest in politics and loved peace. She regularly visited Wales and was met with enthusiasm by the Welsh people. Her death in 1901 was seen by many as the end of an era.

Victoria's reign had been a time of increased industrialisation for Wales – particularly in coal mining and steel producing which had both developed significantly and this proved crucial for the Welsh economy. As well as coal mining, slate, gold and different metal ores were also mined in the South Wales Valleys as it had been found to be one of the richest plains in the world. The two largest slate quarries in the world were located in Wales at Penrhyn and Dinorwig and the Oakley slate mine at Blaenau Festiniog was the largest slate mine in the world. Welsh slate proved a very popular commodity for roofing, floors and tombstones.

Life for the Welsh miners was hard with long hours and many dangers – injury and even death were not unusual. The miners were often discontented but continued working hard – this is one of the popular songs from the period that they sang at the coal face and interestingly, it is in a mixture of English and Welsh- -

I am a little collier and gweithio underground

The raff will never torri when I go up and down

It's bara when I'm hungry

And cwrw when I'm dry

It's gwely when I'm tired

And nefoedd when I die

The complete English translation of the lyrics of the song are as follows:

I am a little collier and working underground

The rope will never break when I go up and down

It's bread when I'm hungry

And beer when I'm dry

It's bed when I'm tired

And heaven when I die

(Wikipedia contributors, 2024)

King Edward VII (1901-1910)

Edward was the eldest son of Queen Victoria. He was an elderly man when he was crowned king. Victoria had blamed Edward (who was nicknamed 'Bertie') for his father's death as he had been a very rebellious young prince. As the Queen's eldest son, Edward, had been bestowed the title Prince of Wales. He did make several visits to Wales for ceremonial events steeped in Welsh culture.

The nine years of Edward's reign were not easy ones for the Welsh. Although the country saw continuing industrial growth, there were both political and social unrest with a number of labour strikes and a rise in Welsh nationalism.

The labour strikes were mainly in the coal mining industry to highlight the poor working conditions.

Despite the social and political unrest, Edward VII did make efforts to maintain unity with Wales. His trips to Wales were to boost morale and highlight the importance of loyalty to the crown. As well as the ceremonial occasions, he also made inspections of  the most important industrial sites but did little to ease the discontent. As he spoke fluent French and German, he preferred to devote his time to touring Europe. In doing so, he did not appreciate that there were growing aspirations for greater self-governance amongst the Welsh.

King George V (1910-1936) and the war years

Throughout his reign, George V made great efforts to maintain unity and stability in Wales. He regularly visited the country to boost morale and to emphasise the importance of national unity.

Thousands of Welsh go to war

The First World War (1914-1918) had a profound impact on Wales – both because of its contribution to the British war effort and its effects on Welsh society. Wales made a significant contribution to the war as thousands of Welsh men were enlisted into the British armed forces and filled many key roles across all three services. Welsh soldiers fought on the Western Front, in Gallipoli, Mesopotamia and all the main areas of conflict. There was a heavy toll on the Welsh soldiers and thousands were killed, wounded or missing in action. Every community in Wales was impacted and mourning the loss of loved ones and the effects of the war were both profound and long-lasting.

Industrial output is increased for the war effort

Wales also played a key role with its industrial output. Welsh coal and steel was vital and production for both was rapidly increased - with many more workers being taken on for both industries. The Welsh steelworks contributed hugely to the production of munitions.

and other war materials.

The experience of the war strengthened

Welsh identity within the United Kingdom and the sacrifice of its soldiers was commemorated in poetry, literature and art.

Hedd Wyn was a popular Welsh poet who was killed in the war Hedd Wyn – whose real name was Ellis Humphrey Evans - wrote his poems in Welsh. He was posthumously awarded the Bard's Chair at the 1917 National Eisteddfod of Wales for his poem Yr Arwr – meaning' The Hero'. Hedd Wyn was killed at the Battle of Passchendaele and his death was seen as a symbol of the loss and tragedy caused by the war.

David Jones was another Welsh artist and poet, who served in World War I and his experiences on the Western Front influenced his work. His epic poem 'Parenthesis' is considered one of the finest literary works of the period. Another leading poet was Wilfred Owen who was born in England but grew up in Birkenhead. Today, Wilfred Owen is regarded as one of the leading war poets and he is also known for his powerful anti-war works.

In the years following the war, there was an increasing desire in Wales for the national identity to be redefined and for greater self-governance to be re-introduced.

David Lloyd George champions the Welsh cause

David Lloyd George became British Prime Minister in 1916 and led the nation through the latter years of the war and in the aftermath. He was born in Manchester but had strong Welsh roots. He passionately wanted Wales to be properly recognised within the United Kingdom and he played a significant role in helping to establish the country's political identity. He advocated greater self governance for Wales and greater recognition of the country's important cultural and historical heritage.

The Labour Party comes to Wales

The English Labour Party was founded in 1900 as a result of the merger of a variety of organisations and trade unions. Wales had always played a significant role in the labour movement, advocating for workers' rights and social reforms. The Labour Party's strength and influence gathered momentum in Wales and in the years between the wars, the Labour Party became one of the main political forces. The Welsh electorate liked what Labour was saying about workers' rights, healthcare and education and soon gave their backing to the new political party.

CHAPTER 11
THE MID-20TH CENTURY AND WAR ON THE HORIZON

George VI never expected to be king as his brother, Edward VIII had been crowned King in January 1936 on the death of their father, George V. However, Edward VIII's reign was a short-lived one as he abdicated the throne just 11 months later- on 11 December 1936- so that he could marry the American divorcée, Wallis Simpson. His abdication caused a constitutional crisis that affected the whole of the UK – including Wales – because it raised questions about the modern role of the monarchy and the stability of the nation. His abdication came at a time when there was significant social and political change in the years leading to the start of World War II.

George VI (1936- 1952)

The reign of George VI was a challenging one with the huge impact of World War II plus the decline of the British Empire and continuing social changes. His coronation in 1937 was a huge event that captured everyone's imagination and was important as it symbolised stability and continuity in an increasingly unsettled world.

The king made a number of visits to Wales during his reign – particularly during the war years to provide crucial moral support, to strengthen the ties between the monarchy and the Welsh people and to demonstrate the relevance of the monarchy during times of uncertainty.

Post war there were a number of social changes in Wales including the decline of the traditional industries such as coal mining and the emergence of new trades. George VI coincided his visits with these changes so that he could spend time talking to the workers who were affected.

World War II (1939-1945)

Everyone in the United Kingdom was involved in the war and made significant contributions to the war effort. When Adolf Hitler invaded Poland in September 1939, Britain and France declared war on Germany. Over the following six years, the war took more lives and destroyed more land and property than any other conflict in history.

Welsh servicemen served in all three branches of the British Armed Forces- the Royal Navy, British Army and the Royal Air Force (RAF). The Welsh regiments including the Royal Welsh Fusiliers (the oldest Welsh regiment), the Welsh Guards and the South Wales Borderers all played crucial roles in conflicts and a number of key battles:

The Battle of Dunkirk

Welsh soldiers along with other British forces were involved in the evacuation of Allied troops from the beaches of Dunkirk in 1940.

The Battle of Britain

Welsh RAF pilots took part in the 1940 operation defending British airspace from German Luftwaffe pilots.

North Africa Campaign

The Royal Welsh Fusiliers served in North Africa and fought in the battles of El Alamein and Tobruk. The South Wales Borderers also saw action in North Africa and were in the Battle of Gazala and the second Battle of El Alamein. Although the Welsh Guards was an infantry regiment used primarily for ceremonial duties, the regiment fought in several battles including the Battle of Tunis. The contribution made by Welsh soldiers fighting against the Germans and Italians, helped to secure victory for the Allied Forces.

Many Welsh soldiers distinguished themselves with great acts of bravery and heroism and were presented with the Victoria Cross and Military Cross in recognition of this.

At home in Wales

The Welsh communities also made great contributions in civil defence, air raid precautions and supporting evacuees. Welsh industries played a vital role in supplying materials for the war effort including coals for ships and steel for weapons and machinery. The Welsh workforce increased  production during the war years and many of the workers were women.

World War writers and poets

There were a number of Welsh writers and poets who contributed to the cultural heritage of Wales both during and after the war. Their work gives a clear insight into the human horrors and experiences of war and its aftermath. Dylan Thomas had been writing poetry and prose prior to the war and became a BBC scriptwriter during the war years to provide information to the public – and importantly, boost morale.

Alun Lewis served as an officer in the British Army during the war and his works reflect his experiences. As a poet he is known for his honesty and depth of emotions. Sadly, he was killed in action in Burma in 1944.

Vernon Watkins was another Welsh poet who was a friend of Dylan Thomas. He too served in the British Army and wrote poetry throughout the war years, exploring many different themes including love and nature as well as his war experiences. Gwyn Thomas was a Welsh writer and his short stories and plays were popular. During the war he worked as a teacher and served in the Home Guard so much of his writing reflects the realities of life in Wales and the impact on the community of the war.

Elizabeth II (1953- 2022)

Queen Elizabeth II's reign was one of the longest and most remarkable in the history of Great Britain. Over the years there were huge social, cultural and political changes, both in Wales and the rest of the UK

Elizabeth II was proclaimed Queen on the death of her father in February 1952. She was crowned in June 1953 when everyone was still rebuilding their lives in the aftermath of World War II. In the years that followed there were huge advancements in technology with the invention of the television and internet and digital communication – all of these completely changed everyday lives. Elizabeth embraced all the new technology, whilst working hard to maintain the traditions of the monarchy.

There were many political changes during Elizabeth's reign too, with the decolonisation of many former British colonies. Amongst the many former colonies to gain independence were India and Pakistan, which both gained independence in August 1947, Sri Lanka (formerly Ceylon) in 1948 and Uganda, Jamaica, Trinidad and Tobago all gained their independence in 1962.

During Elizabeth's reign, the European Union was created and gathered momentum. The United Kingdom joined the EU on 1 January 1973, but following a referendum, left in 2020. There was also the devolution of powers within the United Kingdom of Wales, Scotland and Northern Ireland. From 1998, all these countries were governed independently.

Elizabeth II was a significant cultural figure who represented continuity and stability in a fast-changing world. She regularly travelled abroad to visit countries in the Commonwealth and gave a number of key speeches. She was also Patron of a variety of cultural institutions. She and her husband, Philip, Duke of Edinburgh, had four children. Their marriages were great state occasions, but Elizabeth's reign was also marked by the breakdown of three of her children's marriages and the tragic death of her former daughter-in-law, Diana, Princess of Wales. Throughout her reign, the Queen remained dedicated to her duties and responsibilities as monarch.

(Face of Queen Elizabeth in Twenty Pound Sterling Banknote)

Queen Elizabeth II celebrated her Golden

Jubilee, marking 50 years on the throne in 2002 and her Diamond Jubilee (60 years) in 2012 – both occasions were times for national celebration. When she died, she left a lasting legacy both in the UK and around the world.

The Welsh Language Act –1967

There had been growing concerns about the decline in the use of the Welsh language and the aim of The Welsh Language Act of 1967 was a piece of legislation that was passed to recognise, protect and promote the Welsh Language in a number of ways. It was significant to Welsh people because it recognised the cultural importance of the Welsh language and was viewed as a major step in its preservation and its promotion among the younger generations.

Equality of status:

The Act recognised the equal validity of Welsh with English for legal purposes. This meant that all legal documents could be presented in Welsh.

- Official documents and publications: All literature published by public bodies in Wales should be available in both Welsh and English.
- Education: An emphasis would be placed on the teaching of Welsh in

schools and the use of Welsh in educational settings.

- Public Services: All public services such as health and local government should be conducted in Welsh whenever there was a significant demand.

The Investiture of the Prince of Wales- 1969

On 1 July 1969 there was a magnificent investiture ceremony at Caernarfon Castle where Elizabeth II bestowed the title on her eldest son, Charles (now Charles III). Charles became the 21st Prince of Wales and the ceremony was watched on television by 500 million people worldwide. In anticipation of his new role, Charles had learnt Welsh when he was younger. There had not been a Prince of Wales since 1911. The investiture faced huge opposition from Welsh nationalists who felt that an English prince was being thrust upon them.

Consequently, when Prince William became Prince of Wales on the death of his grandmother Elizabeth II in September 2022, there was no investiture ceremony to avoid any tension. Like his father, Prince William studied Welsh as a teenager in preparation for his future role.

Duties of the Prince of Wales

- To represent the monarch at a variety of different ceremonies and events.
- To maintain and promote the Royal traditions.
- Promote British interests both at home and overseas and enhance business, cultural and diplomatic exchanges.
- To support charitable organisations and initiatives – with emphasis on education, youth development, healthcare and environmental conservation.

The roles of the Prince of Wales in modern times have become far reaching and are seen as important for preparing the Prince of Wales for his future leadership  role both within the Royal Family and worldwide.

(Wikipedia contributors, 2024a)

The Welsh miners' strikes

There were several Welsh miners' strikes and the two main ones took place in 1972 and

1984- 1985. They had significant social, economic and political repercussions not only on the coal mining industry, but numerous mining communities in Wales and the wider labour movement. The strikes have left their mark on the memories of the Welsh mining communities.

The 1972 strike

This dispute started in early January following a dispute over wages. The National Union of Mineworkers (NUM) had demanded a substantial increase in wages and an improvement in working conditions. The aim of the strike was to improve both wages and working conditions for all coal miners in the UK.

The strike lasted seven weeks and resulted in a significant pay increase for miners and an improvement in working conditions and safety standards.

The 1984- 1985 strike

This strike was caused by the announcement made by Margaret Thatcher, the Prime Minister, that 20 coal mines would be closing as they were unprofitable and that the coal industry would be restructured. There was much anger amongst the Welsh miners and fear of job losses in the mining communities.

The aims of the strike were to oppose the closure of the mines and protect both the coal industry and thousands of jobs. The strike lasted nearly a year and was unsuccessful because Mrs Thatcher was determined to break the strike and the NUM lost valuable financial support from other unions. The miners returned to work, but the coal mining industry declined even further.

New industries for Wales

Following the decline of coal mining, a number of new industries began in Wales, and these helped to diversify the economy.

Manufacturing and engineering

There has been significant growth in advanced engineering and manufacturing in Wales – particularly in the aerospace, car and electronic sectors. Companies such as Airbus, Toyota and Dynamics have all opened factories in Wales providing many skilled employment opportunities.

Information technology and digital

Wales has seen growth in both these sectors in recent years. Technology parks have been developed near cities like Cardiff, Swansea and Newport, with companies involved in software development, digital media and telecommunications. All these new industries are currently thriving.

Life sciences and healthcare

The science sector in Wales is rapidly developing with the arrival of new specialist companies in pharmaceuticals, biotechnology and medical devices. Welsh research institutions and universities are driving innovation and development in the sector.

The creative industries

Wales has a vibrant creative industry including film and television production, animation, gaming and design. Today, Cardiff is the hub for media companies with the BBC and other broadcasters all having studios located in the city.

Tourism

With its natural beauty, numerous historic

sites and cultural attractions, tourism has in recent years become an important industry and a significant contributor to the Welsh economy – especially in rural areas. Wales attracts many special interest visitors who enjoy a wide range of interests including cycling, hiking and ornithology. Currently, there are a number of new initiatives promoting sustainable tourism.

Wales joins the European Union- 1973

As part of the United Kingdom, Wales joined the EU on 1 January 1973 and saw both positive and negative impacts from its membership. A significant and very positive aspect was the amount of funding that Wales received from the EU. Various EU funds have provided financial support for economic development, the improvement of infrastructure and job creation.

The EU also provided funding for urban regeneration to help revitalise communities to improve living conditions. Infrastructure of roads, railways and ports was enhanced providing Wales with better connections with other parts of the UK and Europe. The EU also helped to enhance training opportunities to develop skills in the workforce to ensure that they were both more employable and more competitive.

Agriculture and farmers also received EU funding to promote sustainable farming practices. The EU encouraged environmental protection policies and initiated changes to address climate change and preserve biodiversity. The challenges of being a member of the EU included regulatory alignment and immigration. The impact of joining the EU was certainly multi-faceted.

On 23 June 2016, a referendum was held in the UK asking voters whether the UK should remain a member of the European Union or not. In Wales, 52.5% of voters voted in favour of leaving the EU. This result was in line with the rest of the UK where 51.9% voted to leave. This decision has had significant political, economic and social ramifications for Wales – like the rest of the UK - and triggered negotiations with the EU to establish a new working relationship between the UK and EU.

CHAPTER 12

MODERN WALES AND DEVOLUTION

The devolution of powers to Wales took place steadily over several years. The National Assembly for Wales was established in 1999 and was a key moment for the country. Here are the various stages of the Welsh devolution.

The Welsh referendum

In 1997 a referendum was held in Wales and the majority of voters supported the establishment of a National Assembly with devolved powers.

1999 and the National Assembly is established

The National Assembly was officially established in 1999 but had limited legislative powers. It could make secondary legislation and oversee such areas as health, education and local government.

2014, The Wales Act

This act introduced significant changes by granting additional powers to the National Assembly. For the first time, the National Assembly could pass legislation in certain areas without seeking approval from the UK parliament. The Act also paved the way for the devolution of taxation powers so that the Welsh Government could set its own tax rates.

2020 The renaming of the National Assembly

Following the Welsh Parliament and Elections Act that was passed in 2020, the National Assembly was renamed the Senedd Cymru – meaning 'Welsh Parliament'. The act also gave the Welsh Parliament greater powers over transportation, energy and the environment.

Devolution has been warmly welcomed by the Welsh as they feel it gives them greater control over domestic affairs and policies. The Welsh Parliament can make decisions tailored to the specific needs of the Welsh population. Welsh devolution has also contributed to the preservation of Welsh culture, language and identity which in turn has strengthened the sense of Welsh unity.

Key Welsh politicians in the 20th century

Mention has already been made of David Lloyd George who has been the only Welshman to be Prime Minister, but a number of other Welsh politicians played prominent roles during the 20th century.

Aneurin Bevan (1897-1960)

Bevan was a very strong figure in the Labour Party and was the architect of the National Health Service (NHS). He was Minister of Health in the post war Labour government. The NHS was launched in 1948, providing free healthcare to all – regardless of status.

Gwynfor Evans (1912-2005)

Evans was a prominent Welsh nationalist who became the first President of Plais Cymru – the Welsh party. He played a leading role in the Welsh nationalist movement and did much to promote Welsh language and culture. He was a strong advocate for self-government and devolution for Wales.

Clement Davies (1184- 1962)

Davies was the leader of the Liberal Party between 1945-1956. He played an important part in rebuilding the party after World War II and was a keen advocate for progressive politics and civil liberties.

Neil Kinnock

Born in Tredegar in Wales, the only child of a former coal miner, Neil Kinnock was leader of the Labour Party between 1983-1992. He played a central role in modernising the party and moving it towards  the political centre. He was not successful in leading the Labour Party to victory in the general elections, but paved the way to success for Tony Blair and the continuing transformation of the Labour Party

More recently, other Welsh figures who can be added to this list include Rhodri Morgan and Carwyn Jones who have both been First Ministers of Wales since devolution.

Welsh personalities in the 20th century

Dylan Thomas (1914- 1953)

This poet's name is the one everyone mentions when asked the question to name a great Welshman! He was born in Swansea in 1914 and is considered one of the greatest poets and writers of the 20th century. His work is well known for its vivid imagery and emotional depth.

Dylan Thomas received great acclaim early on for his collections of poetry including 18 Poems (1934) and Death and Entrances (1946). In these volumes he explored the themes of life, death and the passage of time. He also made a number of radio broadcasts and Under Milk Wood which captures the lives of people living in a fictional Welsh town.

Unfortunately, Thomas had a troubled relationship with alcohol which led to his premature death when he was aged just 39 years. His influence on modern poetry has been profound and his evocative verse has inspired both readers and writers the world over.

(Wikipedia contributors, 2024a)

Roald Dahl (1916-1990)

One of the world's most beloved children's authors is Roald Dahl. Dahl was born in Llandaff, Cardiff to Norwegian parents. During World War II, he served as a fighter pilot with the Royal Air Force. In the years that followed he became well known for his imaginative and whimsical stories. Today his work is enjoyed by readers aged nine- 90! Many of his books including Charlie and the Chocolate Factory, Matilda and The BFG have been made into successful films. His books have sold more than 325 million copies around the world.

(Wikipedia contributors, 2024d)

Richard Burton (1925 -1984)

Richard Burton was born in Pontrhydyfen and became a highly acclaimed Welsh actor – both on stage and screen. He starred in numerous films including Cleopatra, Who's Afraid of Virginia Woolf? and The Spy who Came in from the Cold. Richard Burton became almost as well-known with the public for his turbulent relationship with his second wife, Elizabeth Taylor – whom he married twice!

Laura Ashley (1925- 1985)

World famous for her quintessentially British style and fabric designs, Laura Ashley was born Laura Mountney in Dowlais, Merthyr Tydfil in 1925. She founded the iconic 'Laura Ashley' brand which is well known for its timeless floral prints and stylish traditional furniture. Over the years, the name Laura Ashley has become a global symbol of British fashion and furniture.

Sir Tom Jones OBE (Born 1940)

Well known for his powerful voice and charismatic presence, Tom Jones was born in Treforest, Pontypridd. During the 1960s he had a string of hit records including It's Not Unusual and Delilah and What's New Pussycat which was the theme song for the James Bond film Thunderball. In 1999 he was awarded the OBE and in 2006 he was knighted by Queen Elizabeth II for his services to music. Although now in his 80s, Tom Jones still regularly appears in shows.

Shirley Bassey (Born 1937-)

Known for her distinctive voice and glamorous looks, Dame Shirley Bassey has fanned the world over. She has many memorable songs to her credit including the

James Bond themes Goldfinger, Diamonds are Forever and Moonraker. She was born in Tiger Bay near Cardiff in 1937 and started performing as a teenager. She was the first Welsh person to reach the No 1 slot in the British charts with As I Love You. With the release of her most recent album, I Owe it All to You in 2020, she is the first female artist to have an album in the UK Albums Chart in seven consecutive decades. She became a Dame Commander of the British Empire in 2020. In 2022 and 2023, commemorative coins and stamps were issued in the UK in her honour.

(Wikipedia contributors, 2024c)

Charlotte Church (Born 1986)

In the late 1990s, Charlotte Church first gained widespread recognition for her angelic soprano singing voice when she was just 12 years old. Church was born in Llandaff, Cardiff. She captivated audiences with her classical repertoire and was the youngest person ever to reach Number 1 in the UK's classical music chart. Since then, she has successfully broadened her appeal as a classical crossover artist, experimenting with pop music. She still lives in rural France and runs a wellness retreat and works in broadcasting.

(Wikipedia contributors, 2024a)

Everyday life in Wales during the 20th century

Everyday life in Wales changed significantly during the 20th century due to various economic, social and political developments.

At the beginning of the century, Wales was very reliant on coal mining and other heavy industries – especially in the South Wales valleys. Communities and everyday life revolved around the coal mines. By halfway through the century, the coal mining had started to decline and younger people in the mining communities moved to the cities in search of work. All the urban communities enlarged in size and many of the mining communities became fragmented.

The Welsh mining villages underwent huge changes with the pit closures. Many villages faced financial hardship as jobs disappeared. Mining had been the primary source of employment for generations and many older people did not want to relocate to the cities but knew they faced unemployment and financial insecurity. When the mines closed there were implications for the health and well-being of the community, but luckily, free healthcare was available to all because of the inception of the NHS.

Education remained very important in Wales and the Welsh language saw a great revival in schools and efforts to promote bibilingualism. The University of Wales had been founded in 1893, but during the 20th century it grew to include a number of different colleges and constitutions. The university also underwent significant restructuring with some of the colleges becoming independent universities.

The 20th century Welsh cultural revival

Known as Y Diwygiad, this was a rhyme with interest in - and a celebration of – Welsh language, literature and music. All these elements help to bolster Welsh national identity. The movement started because it was felt that social and economic changes were threatening the survival of the Welsh language and its culture.

Revitalisation of the Welsh language

One of the main aims of the cultural revival was the revitalisation of the Welsh language (Cymraeg)There were renewed efforts to use

Welsh in schools and to promote its use in literature, the media and everyday life. The Welsh Language Society – Cymdeithas yr Iaith Gymraeg- campaigned for the use of Welsh in public life too.

S4C (Sianel Pedwar Cymru) – Channel Four Wales - is the Welsh-language television channel and during the cultural renaissance it too enjoyed an increased number of viewers and played a significant role in promoting bilingualism. It still primarily broadcasts in Welsh, but it does also have some content in English- particularly news and current affairs.

Literature and poetry

The Welsh literary scene enjoyed a huge revival with writers and poets exploring the Welsh language and a variety of themes. Dylan Thomas has been the most celebrated poet and writer in the 20th century (there is more information on him in the section Welsh Personalities in the 20th century). This was a time with many notable Welsh poets, including R.S. Thomas, Waldo Williams and T.H. Parry-Williams. R.S. Thomas was an Anglican priest whose poems often spoke of the Welsh landscape and reflected on the complexities of modern life.

Gwynn Thomas was a popular novelist and

who portrayed working class life
our and compassion.

music traditions

Welsh folk music and traditions enjoyed a renaissance too. Musicians and singers revived all the Welsh folk songs and hymns and rediscovered the rich musical heritage of Wales. The Eisteddfodau – the annual Welsh festivals promoted Welsh culture and also celebrated its renaissance.

Other genres of Music

Alan Hoddinott (1929- 2008)

Alan Hoddinott was a leading Welsh composer during the 20th century and his work ranged from orchestral to chamber music. He often drew on popular Welsh themes and folklore.

Karl Jenkins (Born 1944)

This highly acclaimed Welsh composer was born in Penclawdd in 1944. At first, he won acclaim as a jazz and jazz-rock musician, but later transitioned to become a classical music composer. He has a very distinctive style which includes elements of jazz, world music and ethnic influences. One of his most famous works is 'Adiemus' which is a series of vocal compositions. Over the years, Jenkins has written music scores for commercials, films and television. In 2015 he was knighted by Queen Elizabeth II.

The Arts

Welsh artists also enjoyed new interest in their work. Favourite themes in their paintings included the local countryside, Welsh history and folklore. Augustus John (1878-1961) was one of the best-known artists of the time and his work spanned the end of the 19th century and the beginning of the 20th century. His influence has lasted much longer. (also refer to the section Welsh Arts in the 19th century)

Kyffin Williams (1918-2006) was a landscape painter who captured the ruggedness of the Welsh countryside in a very distinctive style which was characterised by bold brushstrokes and the use of a sombre colour palette. Ceri Richards (1903-1971) was a popular modernist painter and printmaker who also drew inspiration from the Welsh countryside and mythology for his work.

Theatre

The Welsh National Theatre – Theatr Genedlaethol Cymru- was founded in the capital city of Cardiff. Today the company's main performance venue is located in the Wales Millennium Centre, which is a well-known landmark that overlooks Cardiff Bay.

A number of performances proved particularly popular in the late 20th century, and these included various works by Dylan Thomas and 'How Green was my Valley by Richard Llewellyn, which is based on the 1939 novel with the same name. The company also performed On the Back Hill, based on the 1982 novel by Bruce Chatwin. The novel follows the lives of twin brothers working on a farm in the Welsh borders.

Over the years, The Welsh National Theatre has regularly staged productions of Welsh language plays including adaptations of classical works and contemporary plays that all explore Welsh culture.

Dance

Wales has its own excellent dance company – the National Dance Company Wales (NDC Wales). The NDC Wales was founded in Cardiff in 1983 and is well known for its innovative and diverse productions. The company does not focus exclusively on ballet, but it does include elements of ballet in its repertoire with contemporary dance styles. The company often collaborates with Welsh dancers and choreographers as well as many from all over the world. NDC Wales also goes on international tours to showcase the talented dancers of Wales.

Great Welsh inventors in the 20th century

Thomas 'Carbide' Williams (1860- 1915)

Williams was born in Canada to Welsh parents and his work straddled the end of the19th and beginning of the 20th century. His greatest invention was the process for producing calcium carbide and this was instrumental in the development of the acetylene gas industry.

Griffith Pugh (1909-1994)

This Welsh physiologist and inventor made significant contributions to the science of human survival in extreme weather conditions.

He developed specialist clothing and equipment for mountaineers and his inventions included the down suit and innovative oxygen equipment for use at high altitudes.

Sir Clive Sinclair (1940- 2021)

Sir Clive Sinclair was a prolific inventor whose name became a household name. He was born in London, and he had Welsh grandparents. His best-known invention was the ZX Spectrum home computer and a number of different  consumer electronics. Sinclair also invented the pocket calculator. He made several models that would easily fit in the pocket and was keen that they were cheaply priced and affordable to many-

Sinclair invented the pocket calculator but was best known for popularising the home computer, bringing it to British high-street stores at relatively affordable prices.

The Guardian Newspaper (Siddique, 2021)

Gordon Edge (Born 1952)

Gordon Edge is a contemporary inventor

who has become well known for his pioneering work in wind energy. He has developed variable– speed wind turbines and these have significantly increased the efficiency and reliability of wind power generators.

CHAPTER 13
WALES IN THE EARLY 21ST CENTURY

The 21st century is going to be an important one for Wales and will reflect the country's ongoing development both within the United Kingdom and as part of the global community.

Devolution and Governance

The early years of the 21st century saw the consolidation of Welsh devolution with further powers being transferred to the Senedd (Welsh Parliament) by the UK government.

In 2006, the Government of Wales Act was passed providing the Senedd with greater legislative powers.

2016 – the year of Brexit

The UK's decision to leave the European Union in 2016 had significant implications for

Wales, as the country had received significant EU funding for a series of development projects. The post-Brexit years certainly brought challenges for Welsh trade and agriculture as well as regional funding.

Wales is continuing to make the transition from its reliance on heavy industries like coal mining to new sectors such as technology, renewable energy and service industries. This has become more necessary as new customers must be found post-Brexit.

Rhodi Morgan was the First Minister of Wales between 2000- 2009 and helped to shape the nation's policies and structure of governance in the early years of Welsh devolution. Leanne Wood who is the former leader of Plaid Cymru has also been an influential figure in Welsh politics – advocating further powers of devolution and for social justice.

The impact of COVID-19

The pandemic had a significant impact on Wales affecting both the economy and daily life. The economic disruption led to job losses, business closures and financial hardship for many families. Schools and universities were forced to close and learning went online. Remote learning caused challenges for teachers, parents and students. Social distancing brought loneliness to many Welsh people. Wales implemented a vaccination programme to slow the spread of COVID-19.

Looking to the future

Following Devolution, Wales began a socio-economic revitalisation that would address some of the country's long-standing problems and also seize new opportunities. The Welsh Government outlined ambitious goals that would boost the country's economy, enhance its public services, enrich its culture and promote environmental sustainability.

The key initiatives for the 21st century that were defined

Further economic diversification

Wales needed to further reduce its reliance on the traditional heavy industries such as coal mining and to focus strongly on innovative technological, service and creative industries. The country needs to continue to try and attract new businesses to the area and stimulate economic growth across the country.

The development of education standards and new skills

The importance of education and its link with economic prosperity has been recognised and there have been a number of initiatives to improve standards in schools and provide lifelong learning opportunities. There has been great investment in several vocational training and apprenticeship programmes to help equip school leavers with the required skills for the evolving Welsh job scene.

Health and wellness

Since Devolution, the Welsh Government has been keen to address public health challenges and promote wellness. It has also worked hard to reduce regional inequalities in the health system and to  improve the level of healthcare for everyone. New initiatives have recently been made to tackle current issues including obesity, mental health and substance abuse.

Further promotion of the Welsh culture

This has been an ongoing aim for many years along with the promotion of the Welsh language, arts and traditions. There has been increasing financial support for the various Welsh festivals and cultural programmes. This is important as it not only fosters national pride in Wales, it is also key in promoting both tourism and investment in the country.

More sport for Wales

Rugby remains as popular as ever with the Welsh national team achieving great successes in the Six Nations championship and Grand Slam victories in 2005, 2008, 2012 and 2019. The Welsh national team also reached the semi-finals of the Rugby World Cup in both 2011 and 2019. Alun Wyn Jones captioned the Welsh team on many of these occasions and he is one of Wales' most iconic sportsmen.

Wales has also performed well on the football pitch with Gareth Bale gaining national pride through his achievements at club level and as a player in the Welsh national team, for Tottenham Hotspur and Real Madrid. Many of the Welsh sportsmen and women have become role models for the young and great emphasis is being placed by schools on the many health benefits gained from children taking part in sports from a young age.

Developing renewable energy

Wales has become a leading country in renewable energy and has made substantial investments in wind, solar and hydro-electric power and this is contributing to the country's positive efforts to combat climate change.

CONCLUSION

In tracing the colourful and complex tapestry of the history of Wales, one is inevitably drawn into a narrative marked by resilience, cultural richness and a relentless quest for national identity. From its ancient origins to the modern day, Wales has witnessed a myriad of events and characters that have both shaped its destiny and strengthened its national character.

The story of Wales begins in antiquity, with its earliest inhabitants carving out their cultural identity as they thrived in the country's rugged landscapes. Over the centuries, waves of migration, invasions, and conquests have washed upon its shores – each one leaving an indelible footprint on its history. The Roman occupation brought great progress, marked by infrastructure and the first urbanisation. In contrast, the arrival of the Anglo-Saxons ushered in a difficult period of political fragmentation and great strife.

During the mediaeval era Wales emerged as an individual entity for the first time. This was the result of the rise of powerful Welsh princes and the establishment of independent kingdoms. The legendary figure of Owain Glyndŵr symbolised the enduring spirit of Welsh resistance against English dominance, when he led a valiant but unsuccessful rebellion in the 15th century.

The Union of the Crowns in 1603, when James VI of Scotland was crowned James I of England, brought Wales firmly under the authority of the English monarchy. This led to centuries of political and cultural assimilation. In the 18th century, the Industrial Revolution brought profound changes to Wales, as coal mining and heavy industry completely transformed the South Wales landscape and fuelled huge economic growth. This period also brought both social upheaval and exploitation, resulting in years of struggles for the Welsh working class in the coalfields.

Throughout this turbulent history, one constant thread has remained as strong as ever - the Welsh national identity, with its unique language as its cornerstone. Despite concerted efforts to try and suppress it, the Welsh language has endured as a symbol of great cultural pride and strong resistance.

The 20th century witnessed a great renaissance of Welsh nationalism, culminating in the country's devolution in 1999 which gave Wales a greater degree of autonomy.

Today, Wales faces new challenges as it grapples with the challenges of globalisation, environmental sustainability and the preservation of its unique heritage. There are efforts to promote greater bilingualism and preserve linguistic diversity, with the ever increasing usage of the Welsh language. The debates over Welsh independence continue to simmer too and this reflects a renewed sense of confidence and assertiveness in the Welsh people.

In conclusion, delving into the history of Wales, reveals a land brimming with tales of courage and resilience. These have all contributed to the colourful mosaic that has created the country's heritage. From its ancient legends to its modern day successes, Wales captivates the imagination and leaves an indelible mark on those who visit its rugged landscapes.

As visitors end their exploration of Wales, they take with them more than photographs of beautiful countryside. They carry with them the lesson that nurturing cultural traditions, preserving historical monuments whilst fostering a warm spirit of unity, creates a lasting legacy that will inspire many generations to come....

REFERENCES

- Pembrokeshire Coast National Park. (2024c, February 16). Castell Henllys Iron Age Village - Pembrokeshire Coast National Park. https://www.pembrokeshirecoast.wales/castell-henllys/
- Wikipedia contributors. (2023, February 20). List of hillforts in Wales. Wikipedia. https://en.wikipedia.org/wiki/List_of_hillforts_in_Wales
- Who were the Celts? Understanding the history and culture of Celtic tribes. (n.d.). Museum Wales. https://museum.wales/articles/1341/Who-were-the-Celts/
- Britain Express. (n.d.). Celtic Wales - history of Wales in the Iron Age. https://www.britainexpress.com/wales/history/iron-age.htm
- HWb. (n.d.). https://hwb.gov.wales/
- HWb. (n.d.-b). https://hwb.gov.wales/
- Pwpadmin. (2023, March 6). 10 inventions to thank the Roman Empire for. Gray Line - I Love Rome. https://graylinerome.com/10-inventions-thank-roman-empire/
- Roman Wales | Cadw. (n.d.). Cadw. https://cadw.gov.wales/learn/sites-through-centuries/roman-wales
- What is the Offa's Dyke Path? (n.d.). VisitWales.

https://www.visitwales.com/things-do/adventure-and-activities/walking/offas-dyke-walks

- The National Archives. (2023, June 12). Domesday Book - The National Archives. https://www.nationalarchives.gov.uk/help-with-your-research/research-guides/domesday-book/#:

- Historian. (2023, September 9). 10 Facts about the Normans - Have fun with history. Have Fun With History. https://www.havefunwithhistory.com/facts-about-the-normans/

- Britain Express. (n.d.-b). The Statute of Rhuddlan | History of Wales. https://www.britainexpress.com/wales/history/rhuddlan.htm

- Wales in the Middle Ages. (n.d.). https://owain-glyndwr.wales/age_of_the_princes/mediaeval_wales_detail.html

- Jones, D. (2022, August 30). 5 things you (probably) didn't know about the Plantagenets. https://www.historyextra.com/period/plantagenet/5-things-you-probably-didnt-know-about-the-plantagenets/

- 10 Fast facts about the Plantagenets. (n.d.). Sky HISTORY TV Channel. https://www.history.co.uk/shows/britains-bloodiest-dynasty/articles/10-fast-facts-about-the-plantagenets

- Sarah. (2017, August 3). Daily Living in the Middle Ages - Sarah Woodbury. Sarah Woodbury. https://www.sarahwoodbury.com/living-in-the-past/
- The Tudors in Wales | Cadw. (n.d.). Cadw. https://cadw.gov.wales/learn/sites-through-centuries/tudors-wales
- BBC - History - Wales under the Tudors. (2011, February 17). https://www.bbc.co.uk/history/british/tudors/wales_tudors_01.shtml
- Evans, E. (2022, August 30). Stuart Britain: what was life like for ordinary people? https://www.historyextra.com/period/stuart/stuart-britain-what-was-life-like-for-ordinary-people/
- What Jobs did Children do Underground? • Coal Mining and the Victorians • MyLearning. (n.d.). https://www.mylearning.org/stories/coal-mining-and-the-victorians/236?
- Wikipedia contributors. (2024, February 15). Mining in Wales. Wikipedia. https://en.wikipedia.org/wiki/Mining_in_Wales
- Hedd Wyn (1887-1917) - Literature Wales. (2017, June 12). Literature Wales. https://www.literaturewales.org/our-projects/poetry-of-loss/hedd-wyn-1887-1917/
- Wikipedia contributors. (2024a, February

12). Investiture of Charles, Prince of Wales. Wikipedia. https://en.wikipedia.org/wiki/Investiture_ of_Charles,_Prince_of_Wales

- Wikipedia contributors. (2024a, February 9). Dylan Thomas. Wikipedia. https://en.wikipedia.org/wiki/Dylan_Tho mas
- Wikipedia contributors. (2024d, February 20). Roald Dahl. Wikipedia. https://en.wikipedia.org/wiki/Roald_Dahl
- Wikipedia contributors. (2024c, February 14). Shirley Bassey. Wikipedia. https://en.wikipedia.org/wiki/Shirley_Bass ey
- Wikipedia contributors. (2024a, February 6). Charlotte Church. Wikipedia. https://en.wikipedia.org/wiki/Charlotte_C hurch
- Siddique, H. (2021, September 17). Home computing pioneer Sir Clive Sinclair dies aged 81. The Guardian. https://www.theguardian.com/technology/ 2021/sep/16/home-computing-pioneer-sir-clive-sinclair-dies-aged-81

FREE BONUS FROM HBA: EBOOK BUNDLE

Greetings!

First, thank you for reading our books.

Now, we invite you to join our VIP list. As a welcome gift we offer the History & Mythology eBook Bundle below for free. Plus, you can be the first to receive new books and exclusives! <u>Remember it's 100% free to join.</u>

Simply click the link below to join.

Keep up to date with us on:
YouTube: History Brought Alive
Facebook: History Brought Alive
www.historybroughtalive.com

OTHER BOOKS BY HISTORY BROUGHT ALIVE

Available now in Ebook, Paperback, Hardcover, and Audiobook in all regions.

Other books:

For Kids:

 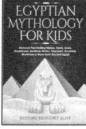 

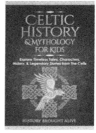  

WALES HISTORY

We sincerely hope you enjoyed our new book *"Wales History"*. We would greatly appreciate your feedback with an honest review at the place of purchase.

First and foremost, we are always looking to grow and improve as a team. It is reassuring to hear what works, as well as receive constructive feedback on what should improve. Second, starting out as an unknown author is exceedingly difficult, and Amazon reviews go a long way toward making the journey out of anonymity possible. Please take a few minutes to write an honest review.

Best regards,

History Brought Alive

http://historybroughtalive.com/

Made in the USA
Middletown, DE
23 March 2025